every man's challenge

Stephen Arterburn
Fred Stoeker with Mike Yorkey

every man's challenge

How Far Are You Willing to Go for God?

WATERBROOK
PRESS

EVERY MAN'S CHALLENGE
PUBLISHED BY WATERBROOK PRESS
12265 Oracle Blvd., Suite 200
Colorado Springs, Colorado 80921
A division of Random House, Inc.

All Scripture quotations, unless otherwise indicated, are taken from the *Holy Bible, New International Version*®. NIV®. Copyright © 1973, 1978, 1984 by International Bible Society. Used by permission of Zondervan Publishing House. All rights reserved. Scripture quotations marked (AMP) are taken from *The Amplified® Bible.* Copyright © 1954, 1958, 1962, 1964, 1965, 1987 by The Lockman Foundation. All rights reserved. Used by permission. (www.Lockman.org). Scripture quotations marked (MSG) are taken from *The Message.* Copyright © 1993, 1994, 1995, 1996, 2000, 2001, 2002. Used by permission of NavPress Publishing Group. Scripture quotations marked (NASB) are taken from the *New American Standard Bible*®. © Copyright The Lockman Foundation 1960, 1962, 1963, 1968, 1971, 1972, 1973, 1975, 1977, 1995. Used by permission. (www.Lockman.org). Scripture quotations marked (NKJV) are taken from the *New King James Version.* Copyright © 1982 by Thomas Nelson, Inc. Used by permission. All rights reserved. Scripture quotations marked (NLT) are taken from the *Holy Bible, New Living Translation,* copyright © 1996. Used by permission of Tyndale House Publishers, Inc., Wheaton, Illinois 60189. All rights reserved.

Italics in Scripture quotations reflect the authors' added emphasis.

Details in some anecdotes and stories have been changed to protect the identities of the persons involved.

ISBN 1-57856-756-4

Published in association with the literary agency of Alive Communications, Inc., 7680 Goddard Street, Suite 200, Colorado Springs, CO 80920.

Library of Congress Cataloging-in-Publication Data
Arterburn, Stephen, 1953–
     Every man's challenge / Stephen Arterburn and Fred Stoeker, with Mike Yorkey.—1st ed.
          p. cm.—(The every man series)
     ISBN 1-57856-756-4
     1. Christian men—Religious life.   I. Stoeker, Fred.   II. Yorkey, Mike.   III. Title. IV. Series.
     BV4528.2.A775 2004
     248.8'42—dc22
                                                                     2003024318

Printed in the United States of America
2005

10 9 8 7 6 5 4

To my loving Father,
who teaches me to say no to ungodliness as I wait for my blessed hope.

———◆———

To Brenda,
I do so love being married to you. What a smile!

———◆———

To Laura and Rebecca,
my cherished daughters and my very worthy sisters in the Lord.
Oh, how I love your laughter!

contents

acknowledgments

The mountains that rose before me as I launched this effort were over-whelming. I nearly turned back at the sight of them all, but there were too many people sustaining me along the way.

Thanks to Steve Arterburn. You were great leading your portions of the climb. Carry on!

Thanks to Mike Yorkey, my trusted Sherpa on this journey. Your encouragement turned our fortunes on a steep slope one shaky afternoon.

Thanks to Steve Cobb, Don Pape, Brian McGinley, Bruce Nygren, Rod Schumacher, Virginia Hairston, and the whole WaterBrook team. It is encouraging to know that if I can just reach the summit, you'll ensure the message reaches my brothers.

Thanks to Vickie Cluney and Ray and Joyce Henderson for praying. You don't just say you'll pray…you do. In the past I counted on my line-man to blow back and hold back my enemies on crisp autumn evenings. Today I count on you as we climb with the mountain goats in this higher league of play. I'm proud to call you my team and honored to call you friends.

And as for that fearsome team of intercessors in Reinbeck, you are in a league of your own. Your work bore the touch of His miraculous right hand. Speaking through you, He strengthened me. Never, ever quit, my friends. You may be toiling in obscurity before men, but the angels can only clasp their hands over their mouths in awe and wonder at the sight of God's work through you. If there is such a thing, I pray that God gives each of you a full author's reward on that great and final day.

Brenda, thank you for praying too. I've no doubt what you can do through Him. As leader of my base camp, your kindness is awesome—I've never seen the like. Jasen, Laura, Rebecca, and Michael—you keep my earthly supply lines moving. Our peace and unity keep me warm and protected on the rocky slopes. May His glory always rest so brightly in you. What fun you are to live with!

And Lord…oh, my! You are my call to climb. How precious You are! How faithful, how kind, how very present! May Your glory shine through this work, and may thousands bend their knees in their homes to give You praise. May Your loving conviction sweep their hearts clean, just as You desire. Thanks for everything, my dearest Friend. As I scaled this range, You reminded me how deeply You cherish each and every one of my brothers. As they read, remind *them,* too. May Your glory abound forever and ever, for You are so worthy.

I felt the electric anticipation as Dave Roever stepped toward the pulpit that Sunday evening. His presence prompted long-dormant passions to bubble inside me, not because of his great evangelist heart, but because he was a Vietnam vet, one of a vast army of American heroes from my childhood days. I grew up adoring soldiers and playing army in my bedroom and around the neighborhood. When I grew older I pored over newspapers for every scrap of military news I could find.

Funny thing, though. As much as I respected and revered those in uniform who served our country, I had never heard a combat veteran speak publicly about his experiences. When I learned that Dave Roever would be speaking at my church, however, I circled the date on the calendar. I wasn't going to miss out on this!

When Dave stepped to the pulpit and turned to face us, my emotions were doused by the reality of what that ugly conflict had done to his body: Dave's disfigurements—heavy skin grafts on the right side of his face and a mouth that was slightly askew—were gut-wrenching to look at. When he set his heavily grafted right hand on the pulpit, however, joy radiated from every skin-grafted cell in his body. My emotions soared as Dave began peeling his story layer by rich layer.

Dave began by describing how he was raised in a godly home, and as high-school graduation loomed in the late sixties, he fervently believed the Lord was calling him into some type of ministry position. Then he received a fateful draft notice in the mail: Uncle Sam was beckoning him to the army. There was a war in Southeast Asia, and tens of thousands of able-bodied young men, eighteen and up, were told they had to go.

Dave wasn't the draft-dodger type. He underwent special-warfare training at the Amphibious Training Center in Coronado, just across the bay from San Diego, and followed that up with more instruction in Northern California at Mare Island's Naval Inshore Operations Training Center. He was trained for riverine warfare, providing transport and standby fire support for Special Forces like the Navy SEALs. Part of the elite Brown Water, Black Berets in the U.S. Navy, Dave and his fellow soldiers were called PBRs, letters that stood for *proud, brave,* and *reliable* because of their fierce, dedicated service. As you might expect from someone who was a passionate Christian, Dave threw his whole heart into his combat training.

When Dave arrived in Vietnam he encountered much more than a war zone. Pornography was everywhere, and R and R for his buddies was a whirlwind of bars, booze, and brothels. The army personnel swore like, well, sailors on leave.

Committing his heart to God, Dave promised to continue seeking after Him and carrying on his devotions and prayer time no matter what. Though Dave expected no one to join him, the last thing he expected was that he would come under friendly fire for taking that stand.

When he read his Bible at night, he was often mocked in the barracks. When he knelt to pray beside his bed, spit rained down on him from the upper bunks. Two men in his unit were especially abusive, pestering him endlessly for his faith. But Dave walked resolutely before God—proud, brave, and reliable.

One bright morning his unit scurried through their work on several rickety river docks deep in the jungle. Suddenly they came under withering fire from the Vietcong. Amid the chaos soldiers scrambled to find cover and direct fire on the enemy.

The rat-a-tat sounds of machine-gun fire and exploding grenades shattered the calm. Dave grabbed a white phosphorous grenade and pulled the pin. Phosphorous grenades aren't your standard-issue grenade. Phosphorous burns with hellish intensity, and water can't put it out. When the burning shrapnel of this horrible weapon pierces the skin, the phosphorous often burns and smolders painfully inside the wound for days.

Dave scampered to put himself in position to lob the grenade at the enemy, but before he could toss it, the grenade exploded six inches from his head, blowing away part of his face and his right hand. Phosphorous splattered across his wounds in scorching, blistering fury. One of the men who had spit on him watched in horror as Dave stumbled in agony and fell into the river, knowing full well the water would not cool his wounds. He watched frantically for Dave to surface again.

Meanwhile, writhing in silent screams beneath the surface, Dave strained for a foothold on the river's bottom as his face burned further away. Launching himself from the muddy bottom with all his might, he burst through the surface, gulped some air, and screamed, "Jesus, I still love You!"

As Dave fell back beneath the waves, the watching soldier was stricken deeply, scrambling instantly to his knees to give his heart to the Lord in the midst of that fierce firefight.

What a witness! Tears flowed from my eyes when I heard his story. *What if that had been me? Would I have responded like that? Would I still have praised God while experiencing excruciating pain?*

In a sense Dave experienced a spiritual pop quiz that fateful morning in Vietnam. You remember pop quizzes from high school: They are a diabolical truth serum used by evil teachers to expose your knowledge (or lack of it) of material you should have studied. You find out how you're doing in class. If the grades are posted, *everyone* finds out how you're doing.

God loves pop quizzes too, but He doesn't use them to test our knowledge. Instead, He tests our character. We get to see what we're really made of, and often those around us get to see it too.

That's what happened in Dave Roever's case, and I have to say, he passed with flying colors, helping to save another man's soul in the process.

I'd been thinking about pop quizzes at the time because I'd just finished a series in a Sunday-morning marriage class that I taught with Brenda. That morning I had shared a pop-quiz story that had happened to me early in our marriage. To set the scene, two years of staggering in-law problems had taken its toll, and our marriage was quickly wilting away.

One Valentine's Day I went to a Hallmark store to buy a card. That's what husbands are supposed to do, right? While rummaging through the card rack, I was hit by one of God's pop quizzes.

Fingering through dozens of cards, I read the texts. One by one I returned them to the rack. I judged them to be too mushy, too contrived, or too romantic. Little by little, panic settled in as I sensed the inevitable. I could not find one Valentine card in the store that I could give Brenda with any measure of sincerity. Our romance was dead, and our marriage was on life support.

Head down, I scurried from the store, recognizing the depth of our loss. My grade on the quiz? Sickening!

But while I flunked that time, my eyes had been opened, and I knew where I stood. I had some character work to do, and it was time to start "studying" my wife.

Still, such quizzes pale next to Dave Roever's. Dave's torturing quiz touched my deepest chords of sympathy, but I considered him lucky, too. He took the ultimate pop quiz and aced it. Most of us never even get to take the quiz.

I mulled over Dave's quiz many times during the next two years. *How would I have done? Man, I'd like to know!* While I didn't relish the thought of pulling the pin on a phosphorous grenade, I wanted to pass some kind of test. I knew in my heart that I'd rather take that test and fail than never be tested at all. One November morning I rolled out of bed to shower and shave, not knowing that examination day was upon me.

I'll never forget that afternoon when the crisp air and sparkling blue sky arched over Iowa. I was tooling along West Des Moines' Eighth Avenue to deliver a package to a client. For some forgotten reason, I was driving Brenda's midnight blue Chevy station wagon that day, the one with the country-squire wood panels that made her feel like Mrs. Brady. But I dearly loved that car, and as with any guy driving a great car on a gorgeous afternoon, everything seemed right in the world. Business was good, and my third child, Rebecca, had just been born two weeks earlier. She was the cutest little Gerber baby on the planet.

Heading south, I approached a familiar intersection: Quality Ford on the left and Jimmy's All-American Café on the right. I glanced down at the speedometer—thirty-five miles per hour—perfect, right on the nose. Things were smooth as a quiet lake on a sweltering midsummer eve.

Suddenly a brand-new, full-sized pickup swerved in front of me. I don't know how he missed seeing me, but he did. Everything happened in a flash. My right foot hit the brake at the instant of impact, locking my knee just in time for the full jamming impact. My shoulder strap failed to catch, and as my upper body flew forward, my left thumb caught the steering wheel, cracking the bone and snapping the ligaments that held it in place. My chest slammed into the steering wheel, which folded like a cheap accordion against the dash. We had collided nearly head-on, and the impact was equivalent to hitting a brick wall at sixty-five miles per hour.

Slumping back against my seat in a stunned, listless daze, I murmured a swear word. Almost at once, sirens whined in the distance. I was amazed at the superhuman response time. "Man, these guys are good," I said to myself.

The light began to fade to gray, and my spirit began to slip away. I felt the moorings of my soul letting go, like the ropes of a great ship loosening and slipping from the pilings of a dock. Everything was so peaceful, so easy, so natural. I remember feeling quite surprised that I felt no trace of doubt. I knew exactly where I was heading—to heaven—and I had no fear. Rolling my head back in that peaceful moment, I remember thinking, *Death isn't such a big deal at all. It's really kind of nice.*

But then, for no apparent reason, my spirit cried out. I began to pray, *Lord, I've done nothing for You yet. I want so much to stay here and do something for You. And, Lord, I want to raise my kids for You and make sure they are okay. They are so young, and I have so much to teach them. I want so badly to know them, and I love Brenda, and she'll be so alone, and now that we have everything working between us, I want to know her and love her and be the husband You wanted me to be.*

My prayers intensified. *Please, Lord, I want to live and serve You here. I don't want to come to heaven empty-handed, with nothing to give You. This all feels so wonderful right now, and I really do want to see You, but I'm not ready to go. Please give me a chance to get You something. Please let me live.*

As quickly as they had begun to slip, the moorings began to tighten again. A new and different peace settled over me. Having long ago memorized a number of hymns during my battle for sexual purity, I now began to praise Him, softly singing hymns in worship.

A female paramedic ripped the door open and, surveying the scene, knew there was no time to lose. She later said that she *knew* I'd never make it to the hospital alive. She'd seen this same situation many times before: My face was ashen gray from the massive internal bleeding in the chest cavity. A check of my blood pressure did nothing to dissuade her. She and other paramedics worked frantically as we sped away, and I heard her call ahead to alert the trauma surgeons. They would have to open my chest immediately upon my arrival at the hospital.

I simply lay there softly singing hymns under my breath and in total peace. The paramedics quickly rolled me into the emergency room. A witness had called Brenda from the accident scene, so she arrived at about the same time I did. A chaplain met her at the door…the same chaplain who'd already put an arm around a young wife earlier that day and told her that her husband didn't make it. He fully expected he'd have to do the same with Brenda.

Pam Behnke, Brenda's best friend, also arrived to lend support. As head of the heart unit at the hospital, she knew the surgeons and had heard the paramedics' fears. She wanted to be there when the chaplain broke the news.

I don't remember much from those first moments in the emergency room. My most vivid memory is staring into the bright lights of the ceiling when suddenly the stricken face of my dear friend Dave Johnson poked into view. He was so scared. He's such a man's man, and I'd never seen him like that. I remember Brenda hovering so tenderly over me with terror in her eyes. Pam stood by, of course. My pastor, Ray Henderson, came by. Everyone was frightened.

But the moorings held fast. The Lord had heard my prayer, and there would be no surgery. A severe blow to the chest can cause a temporary severe drop in blood pressure and traumatic shock, but in my case, there was no internal bleeding. Two hours later I walked out of the hospital under my own power.

I still had a busted thumb that would have to be taken care of. Several days later doctors inserted a pin and wrapped my hand in a cast. The coughs and sneezes that wracked my bruised ribs drove me batty, but I wasn't complaining: I had lived through a life-and-death test.

Looking back, did I ace this exam like Dave Roever? Heavens, no! He beat me hands-down. Remember my reaction to the sudden crash? I muttered a swearword. That hardly ranks with "Jesus, I still love You!" Evidently swearing had not been totally eliminated after eight years of being a Christian.

But that's secondary to what I really learned from the accident. If I were wondering what I was really made of as a Christian deep down, now I knew.

I knew that I loved my wife and kids enough to give up the peace of heaven for their sake, and I knew more than ever that I wanted them to grow up in the knowledge of Christ.

That's what pop quizzes and big final exams do: They tell you what you're made of when the chips are down. They challenge you and prove you.

I can't arrange life's twists and turns to test you—only God can do that. But I can share scriptures that will challenge you like pop quizzes straight from God.

Every Man's Challenge has forty "quizzes" comprised of scriptures, stories, and quiz questions to help you to grow in your sanctification in Christ over forty days. My coauthor, Steve Arterburn, and I hope you pass every one.

Why forty days? Spans of forty days have been monumental throughout the course of history. The purifying rains of Noah fell for forty days. The Law of God was illuminated to Moses over forty days at Sinai. The inspection of the Promised Land by Israeli spies lasted forty days. After the giant Goliath mocked God's armies for forty days, David rose up and slew the enemy. Our Lord Himself was tested forty days in the wilderness, and after the Resurrection, Jesus revealed Himself regularly to His disciples for forty days before ascending to heaven's throne.

I pray that these forty days of inspection will purify you and freshly illuminate God's laws in you so that you will rise up in victory and slay the enemy like David.

I've heard it said that simply recognizing a flaw in your life brings you halfway to victory, but I disagree. I believe that it's our *commitment to obedience* that brings us halfway to victory. If we are committed to obey Christ, then we are at least halfway home, because God has provided us the rest of what we will need for victory:

> His divine power has given us everything we need for life and godliness through our knowledge of him who called us by his own glory and goodness. Through these he has given us his very great and precious promises, so that through them you may participate in the divine nature and escape the corruption in the world caused by evil desires. (2 Peter 1:3-4)

So more than anything, *Every Man's Challenge* will be testing your commitment to obedience. Obedience means everything in a victorious walk in Christ, but failing to yield our will in obedience to Christ stalls our sanctification in this life.

Obedience is the beginning of valor, and we want you to be a man of valor, ready to stand and fight for the truth. We were created to be real men, walking in the image of God.

But when I look around these days, I don't think we're walking too well, and I can assure you that many, many women don't think we're walking very well either. One woman recently sent me this e-mail:

> I am not thinking too highly of men this evening. Do you see very many of them honestly change for the better? I know so many women who have finally given up, letting their husbands do whatever they want. That is not how I want to end up. Otherwise, why be married?
>
> Why does it seem like God allows men to do whatever they please? Women pray for their husbands for years. Why is there so little response? What is the answer?

Is this a rare e-mail? Nope. I get so many of these that it has become a shameful indictment of us as men. Why *is* there so little response in our hearts to our women and children? to God and His Word? What *is* the answer?

It is time to examine ourselves and get with the program:

> Examine yourselves to see whether you are in the faith; test yourselves. Do you not realize that Christ Jesus is in you—unless, of course, you fail the test? (2 Corinthians 13:5)

I'm concerned that we as men are too often satisfied to avoid examination and to stay as we are. Studies show that 83 percent of men will do anything to avoid dealing with problems in their marriages.

We haven't answered God's challenge. Real men don't make their wives pray for them in desperation for years. They change. Real men don't show so little response to their wives' desires. They change. Real men feel horrible when they discover that they've driven their wives to a point where they've simply given up and quit trying. We have no right to stay like this.

Man to man, I challenge you to take some time to examine yourself. You might take these tests alone in the quiet of the morning, or you might take them with a friend in a weekly accountability setting, taking turns asking each other the quiz questions. You might even take the tests as part of a men's small-group study, as many have done with other books in the Every Man series.

However you choose to use *Every Man's Challenge,* the "exam" begins with sections on sin and sexual purity and then moves to an inspection of your family relationships as husband and father. Does that mean this book is only for married guys? Not on your life! If you are single, have no fear. For one thing, if you are not married now, there is a good chance you will be married somewhere down the line. It is never too early to consider your ways and change. But even if you never marry, God's instructions regarding love and selflessness in marriage are easily relevant to other relationships in life.

Along with the exam, *Every Man's Challenge* paints a picture of what the Christian life looks like on the other side of sexual purity. If you've read *Every Man's Battle* and have engaged in the battle, you should be seeking further changes that reflect this step of obedience, changes that will cement your victory over sexual sin.

Just where are you heading on the road of sexual purity? Where *should* you be heading? These are good questions, and that's why *Every Man's Challenge* begins with sexual purity. Not that we'll be rehashing material from *Every Man's Battle,* because we won't. Instead, we'll examine the lessons from the perspective of what we've learned in this battle. We will be discussing how we might apply these lessons in the other areas in our lives.

Maybe you've never really battled with sexual impurity, and you're wondering if you can relate to the material. You have nothing to worry about. You will still be challenged by the picture of what is possible in Christ and what He expects of us.

God's Word is your mirror. When you step before it and look at what you've become, what do you see? You'll find out in the coming pages.

life on the other side of sexual purity

The apostles taught that true salvation should always have the same effect upon believers: It should encourage a conscious rejection of ungodliness and lead to holier living. A profession of Christ must be accompanied by a choice of godly living:

> For the grace of God that brings salvation has appeared to all men. It teaches us to say "No" to ungodliness and worldly passions, and to live self-controlled, upright and godly lives in this present age, while we wait for the blessed hope—the glorious appearing of our great God and Savior, Jesus Christ, who gave himself for us to redeem us from all wickedness and to purify for himself a people that are his very own, eager to do what is good. (Titus 2:11-14)

John went so far as to say:

> We know [absolutely] that anyone born of God does not [deliberately and knowingly] practice committing sin. (1 John 5:18, AMP)

Just where are you in this transformation in Christ? Your sexual purity is one measure. After all, sexual purity is normal for a Christian man. In that sense, are you normal?

If you aren't, you must engage in a transforming battle for sexual purity. As men commit their lives to this battle, we're often asked, "What is life like on the other side of purity? What's it like to be normal in Christ?" Many markers of personal change will emerge as you pass through this battle's crucible, changes with spiritual effects that stretch far beyond your sexuality into every corner of your life.

The first marker is that you'll be more certain of the following truth than ever before: You're as close to the Lord as you want to be. Before the battle you *suspected* that your sexual sin was hurting your intimacy with God. On the other side of the battle, you will be absolutely *certain* that harbored sin creates distance from God. You will be certain, too, that you yourself play a vital role in your own sanctification through your daily decisions.

Your hatred of sin will grow. You may have suspected that you were paying a dear price for your sin before the battle, but you were largely blind to the incalculable losses you were incurring in your life. Now that you are enjoying the freedom on the other side of purity and reveling in its blessings, you know for certain the full price of sin, that it's a silent, grotesque crippler preventing you from walking normally and uprightly in God's image as you were created to do. On the other side, you'll have a deeper urgency to see that all forms of sin are discussed openly and exposed clearly to both the saved and seeker alike so that all might walk normally in His image.

Your hatred of Satan will grow too, as you realize more than ever before that you must personally resist him. Through God's grace and power, you must wrest control of your life from Satan's influences if you are to stand normally in the truth.

friend of the seeker

Son of man, prophesy against the shepherds of Israel; prophesy and say to them, even to the [spiritual] shepherds, Thus says the Lord God: Woe to the [spiritual] shepherds of Israel who feed themselves! Should not the shepherds feed the sheep?...The diseased and weak you have not strengthened, the sick you have not healed, the hurt and crippled you have not bandaged, those gone astray you have not brought back, the lost you have not sought to find.

EZEKIEL 34:2,4, AMP

This is God's eternal, chilling warning to His shepherds, and since Christ has made us "a kingdom and priests" (Revelation 5:10), surely God expects each of us to pay close attention to this warning as well. We must think over these words carefully, because never has sin been more rampant in America than it is today, and the percentage of folks in our pews with little Christian heritage is growing rapidly.

When Brenda and I began teaching premarriage classes in the mideighties, most of the couples were what we called "normal Brad-and-Joni–types"—both partners were clearly committed to purity and Christian ways in the way they lived. By the time we quit teaching premarriage classes a mere twelve years later, I would say that one-third of the couples had lived together prior to marriage and two-thirds had already slept together.

I'll never forget my pastor's exclaiming in frustration, "How can so many people in this church be living this way!"

Good question, and if I had to hazard a guess, I'd say it's because more and more young people are growing up in broken homes where they never hear what God teaches in the Bible. But I also wonder if we haven't gotten scared? As congregations, are we so afraid of hurting our attendance figures that we've stopped telling the hard truth on Sunday mornings in church and Sunday school? As individuals, have we stopped living and telling the truth on the other days of the week for fear of losing our friends and offending our kids? We've left the weak and crippled to limp hopelessly on in their sin, unaware that they aren't walking normally.

As an illustration, for a while I lived in the San Francisco Bay Area, where I liked to hang out on North Broadway, the downtown's adult-theater district (these were the days before I became a believer). I liked ambling by the doorways so I could get a good look at the barely clad busty women standing in the doorways. Whenever they called out, "Hey, big boy, ya wanna come in and play?" they scared me to death. I might have been up to my neck in porn, but I didn't want to know *what* I might find behind those doorway curtains.

But let me ask you something: Can you guess what those women of the night were wearing as they stood in the doorways? Do you suppose that they looked like Caroline Ingalls of *Little House on the Prairie,* with long sleeves to the wrists, collar to the neck, and skirt to the pavement?

Heavens no, they wanted to get your motor running! They were dressed in little spaghetti-strap dresses with hiked-up hemlines, giving you an eyeful of every curve on their bodies.

Recently, in our church, I was quickstepping off to Sunday school. As I came around a corner, I nearly ran head-on into a girl I knew from the youth group. Everything happened so fast. We each braked hard, jolting to a stop and ending up face to face, about two inches apart. She was shorter than me, and when I looked down to apologize, I audibly gasped. Guess what she was wearing? One of those spaghetti-strap dresses, just like the ones I'd left behind in San Francisco.

In amazement, but without a trace of judgment, a thought slammed through my head: *Are our daughters dressing like whores and strippers now?* I meant no harm, but because of my background, that was the first thought that popped through my astonished brain. She didn't even know that what she was doing was wrong. As parents, why aren't we telling the truth? Why aren't we teaching our kids not to dress seductively these days?

Linda grew up in the church and recently approached her youth pastor with a question. "I've been giving oral sex to different boys at our parties for quite a while now. I don't know why, but I just thought I should ask you about it. Is that wrong for me to do?"

Stumbling a bit, the youth pastor asked, "Were these your boyfriends?"

"No, I wasn't dating any of them," she responded. "It's just a casual thing. All the guys know me for it, and that's why they come to the parties. Now they expect it. I feel quite a bit of pressure to keep giving them what they want, because I've become quite popular because of it. Still, I thought maybe I should ask you about it, just to make sure it was okay."

Where were her parents? Her Sunday-school teachers? Her youth-group leaders?

Where are you? We all *know* we should teach some standards of dress and purity in both our homes and our churches, but too often we dawdle and hem and haw and never quite get around to it. We want to be friendly to everyone, and we wouldn't dream of hurting anyone's feelings. But could it be that we've become so friendly that we've forgotten to be their friend?

What is a real friend? A friend tells you the truth about your behavior, even when it's not easy to do. A friend is someone who tells you that you aren't walking normally and, what's more, that you'll never walk normally until you shape up.

We've put in coffee carts and welcome centers to be warm and inviting when the weak and the crippled stagger through our church doors. How can we be so cruel as to hide the truth from them behind these same coffee carts and welcome centers so they never hear it?

I've got nothing against coffee and a relaxed atmosphere at church—I like it. And I'm aware that people are looking for love and acceptance. We all want that.

But it isn't loving to give them only what they want. We must also give them what they need—the truth. When we don't, our church bodies hemorrhage into massive internal bleeding.

We gave a copy of *Every Man's Marriage* to a good Christian friend active in her church and respected as a conservative school-board member in a district across town. After reading several chapters, she burst into tears and stopped reading. "As I read along, the beauty of this picture of marriage only reminded me of what I'd never have with my husband," she explained. "I couldn't stand the pain of reading it any longer."

That's what I mean by internal bleeding. We have all these happy, friendly churches with happy-looking people happily doing work for God, and yet, beneath the surface, nothing is making sense. Husbands aren't sacrificing for holiness and right living, wives are giving up, and behind every whitewashed wall are dead-men's bones.

To be a friend we must define holiness clearly so that we can all walk normally. We did this in *Every Young Man's Battle*, which prompted Kelli to write us this note:

I read your book *Every Young Man's Battle* and have never heard Christians talk so openly about sex. I grew up in church and was always taught that intercourse before marriage was wrong, but that was it. Once a year we went through the True Love Waits program, signed the card, and then didn't talk about it again until the following year. My father even took me out on a date once and gave me a "purity" ring to remind me not to have intercourse, but no one told me that all the other stuff was wrong too. As I think back, I can't help feeling that if half the talks about abstinence in our youth group were about foreplay and total purity instead, I wouldn't have ever gone far enough with a boy to have to worry about intercourse. *Thank you for the truth.*

We are a kingdom and priests. We must each rise up bravely and tell the truth about sin to our kids and to our friends, because only the truth will bring back the straying and strengthen the weak and crippled. People long for the truth, like Kelli. They don't want to limp along. They want to walk normally. They just need someone to tell them.

Yet somewhere along the way, we decided to stop defining holiness too clearly because we didn't want to seem too different from other people, scared of what people might think and scared that we might hurt our relationships at home. Now we have our wish—we don't look much different at all, and we're too often limping along in the same fog as the lost.

Our girls don't know the modest from the sensual or that petting and oral sex are wrong. Our divorce rates equal those of our unsaved friends, and our marriages no more picture Christ's relationship to the church than theirs do. Christian men are just as addicted to pornography as those outside our churches.

Are you strengthening the weak, binding up the crippled, and bringing back the strays? Are you even strengthening yourself, or are you still sucking spiritual milk from baby bottles? The meat of God's Word is necessary for strength, no matter how tough it can be to bite off and chew. Jesus was the Word in flesh, and the life of the Son is in the Word. An encounter with the meat of God's Word, then, is an encounter with Jesus, our Healer and our standard for living. Every touch from His life in the truth of His Word has one purpose, to bring your life up to the normal, higher heights in Him.

There is no healing without hard truth, no matter how nice things look on the outside during the week and no matter how good the coffee smells on Sunday morning. The broken bones must be set, and the torn cartilage repaired, by the truth, or the crippled will never walk normally again.

Quiz

Are you afraid to give your family what it needs because it might make them look too different? Or because it might hurt your relationship with them?

Do you have an active plan for teaching standards to your kids, or are you dawdling?

red flags

What agreement is there between the temple of God and idols?
For we are the temple of the living God. As God has said: "I will
live with them and walk among them, and I will be their God,
and they will be my people."

"Therefore come out from them and be separate, says the
Lord. Touch no unclean thing, and I will receive you. I will be a
Father to you, and you will be my sons and daughters, says the
Lord Almighty."

Since we have these promises, dear friends, let us purify our-
selves from everything that contaminates body and spirit, per-
fecting holiness out of reverence for God.

2 CORINTHIANS 6:16–7:1

If you still have a hint of sexual immorality in your life (see Ephesians 5:3),
some of these red flags could be flapping around in your backyard:

- Do you tell off-color jokes? Do you like coming up with double
  entendres and making wordplays with double-sided sexual
  meaning?
- Do you channel-surf hoping to glimpse something racy on television? Do you catch yourself watching voyeuristic shows like *elimi-
  DATE?*

- If a certain woman at your office calls in sick, do you feel a bit down in the dumps?
- Did your last hiring decision have more to do with her body than her résumé?
- Are you finding your wife to be less sexually satisfying?
- Have you told your wife that she is too overweight to turn you on?
- Do you have sexual interests or behaviors that you can't share with your wife?
- Do you linger over lingerie ads in the newspaper?
- Do you watch women's figure skating or women's beach volleyball on television, although you have little interest in these sports?
- Do you turn on exercise shows just so you can enjoy those closeups of participants' breasts, rear ends, and inner thighs?
- Do you rent videos or go to movies where you can watch other people having sex?
- Do you admire the cute girl passing by, whistling to yourself and saying, "Nice rear"?
- Do you flirt—and know you're doing it?
- Do you communicate deeply with a person of the opposite sex in an Internet chat room?
- When you are making love with your wife, does another face flash across your mind?
- Do you daydream about other women?
- Do you dream about hot scenes with other women at night?
- Do you think about old girlfriends when things aren't going so well at home?

Maybe you chafed and got defensive or angry as you read through this list. Maybe you aren't angry. Maybe you're just appalled. Or perhaps you disagree with the entire premise, like Greg. We received this e-mail from his wife, Cheri:

Though he has read *Every Man's Battle,* my husband, Greg, has bought into the lie that "all men look" because they are visual. He says it is impossible for a *real* man not to look at a babe in a string bikini. He threatened me with divorce if I didn't stop nagging him about this. He also said that if I'm looking for a man who doesn't notice other women, then I'm going to be looking for a long time.

Impossible for a "real" man not to look?

Hmmm. I don't know what that means, but I know one thing—it's not impossible for a *normal* man to live this way.

What do you mean? you're thinking. *Are you saying that I'm abnormal because I like to look at the female body?*

No, I'm not saying that. God is saying that. God doesn't measure normal in relation to the *world.* He measures it in relation to the *Word,* using words like *sin,* which means "missing the mark."

We're talking about the mark set by Jesus. Jesus was the Word in flesh, so He is our mark. When God speaks of normal, He speaks along these lines: *Jesus is My beloved Son, in whom I am well pleased. He is the most normal person ever to walk on planet Earth. You are a Christian, my child. Are you walking normally like My Son, Jesus?*

As Christian men we must measure from this mark. Why? Because becoming normal is what Christianity is all about. If we don't become normal like Jesus, we trample and hurt those around us, especially those we have pledged to love the most. Cheri is clearly pained by her husband's roving-eye behavior:

I am sick to my stomach to think that for the rest of my life, I will be robbed from having fullness from my marriage. This bothers me so much. Greg is so sick of being reminded of how I feel about it, but he does it even more! Can you imagine? Everywhere I go with my husband I know I can't keep his attention...*nowhere!*

Greg may think he's a real man, but it never matters what we think. The real question is: Are you normal according to the Word of God?

Quiz

Are you more sexually pure today than you were a year ago? five years ago?

Are you zealous to perfect your holiness?

being normal

Therefore, my dear friends, as you have always obeyed—not only in my presence, but now much more in my absence—continue to work out your salvation with fear and trembling, for it is God who works in you to will and to act according to his good purpose.

Do everything without complaining or arguing, so that you may become blameless and pure, children of God without fault in a crooked and depraved generation, in which you shine like stars in the universe as you hold out the word of life.

Philippians 2:12-16

What is normal? I'll let Chad explain it, a sixteen-year-old who sent this e-mail:

> Reading *Every Young Man's Battle* really opened my eyes. My girl-friend and I broke up two weeks ago, though it wasn't very easy. Both of us wanted to serve God, but we couldn't keep from having sex, and that sin caused decay in our relationships with God and with each other. We both wanted to be together and serve God together, but the guilt and distance we felt from God were too great.
>
> I never thought of sex as being wrong—as a matter of fact, I was raised to believe it was normal. Everyone seems to do it. But after

reading what you wrote and listening to what God was trying to tell me through the Word, I now understand that it is *not* normal for a Christian to have sex before marriage.

Chad found out that being normal means thinking like God thinks and acting like it. God says it's normal for a Christian guy to keep his way pure (see Psalm 119:9) and to set no vile thing before his eyes (see Psalm 101:3). It's normal for a Christian to avoid lusting after girls (see Job 31:1).

It's normal to have no hint of sexual immorality in your life (see Ephesians 5:3) and for normal conversations to have no trace of coarse language or filthy jokes (see Ephesians 5:4). Normal guys don't leer at breasts and wink at one another with a low whistle as the babes prance by, and they don't rent *Titanic* so they can watch Kate Winslet drop her robe and stretch nude across the couch.

Too often we call God's ways confining and much too hard and tight. Why not just call them what they really are—normal?

We must be fervent and anxious to become normal—as defined by Jesus, not by us. In fact, that is really job one for us, to become blameless and pure in the midst of a crooked and depraved generation so that our witness remains shining and true. I didn't always understand that.

I'll never forget the day when I blasted Brenda with a bellowing frenzy and crushed a hole in the drywall with my bare fist as an exclamation point. Pleased with the drama of my little display, I arrogantly turned back toward her, glaring fiercely.

That was just the latest outburst in a series that began on our wedding night, when I had violently rifled a hairbrush across the room in rage. I lashed out often during our honeymoon in Colorado's Estes Park, even theatrically storming out of our motel room like a raging grizzly bear.

Upon our return to Iowa, Brenda infuriated me when she made a rookie mistake with the laundry: She turned all my white dress shirts a pale pink when she washed them with some reds. I exploded, tearing the shirts into shreds before her eyes. On another occasion she'd dodged a pot of bean soup that I slung across the kitchen floor. On still another, she'd shrunk back in fear when I kicked a hole in another wall during yet another rampage.

By now she'd finally had it. After I punched that hole, rage covered *her* face. Brenda menacingly leaned in and jabbed her finger toward my nose. With a pair of narrowed eyes that would make Clint Eastwood proud, she snapped, "I thought I married a Christian, and I did it for a reason! I didn't want to live with something like this. I don't care what you grew up like; this isn't normal. You are going to fix this temper, or we'll be separated so fast it'll make your head spin. I'm not going to live like this for the rest of my life, and you'd better not doubt me!"

Spinning away, she made her own stormy exit, stage right. I was stunned.

You don't have a right to stay like you are! That thought had never occurred to me before. I don't have a right? I was honestly flabbergasted. I'd been like this all my life.

Where I came from, the louder you were, the righter you were. Unrestrained anger was a hallmark of our home. If you were ticked, you let the whole world know how you felt. Once the explosions were over, you simply swept the emotional wreckage of these tirades under the rug and went about your business as if nothing had happened.

I have baggage! That, too, was a thought that had never occurred to me before, and I didn't much like the sound of it.

Where does she get the right after two months of marriage to dictate changes like this? I huffed. The answer: from God.

Brenda had said, "I thought I married a Christian, and I did it for a reason. I didn't want to live with something like this." God had painted a picture of what a Christian man looks like in the Bible, and Brenda's dad and uncles had lived out that picture before her for twenty years. When I'd claimed Christ as my Lord, she knew what that meant and what to expect. And the truth is, when I claimed Christ, I gave up my right to look any differently, and I gave up my right to all baggage. So did you:

The acts of the sinful nature are obvious:…hatred, discord…fits of rage, selfish ambition, dissensions.…

But the fruit of the Spirit is love, joy, peace, patience, kindness, goodness, faithfulness, gentleness and self-control. Against such things there is no law. Those who belong to Christ Jesus have cruci-fied the sinful nature with its passions and desires. (Galatians 5:19-20,22-24)

This is God's picture of what is normal and what is not. Which looks more like you, the acts or the fruits? I don't know about you, but I was a fraud, and continuing to stonewall any personal change made little sense anymore.

You don't have a right to stay the way you are.

Right here is where sanctification begins. I have to confess that I've never really cared for the word *sanctification*. To me it's a clumsy word, and it seems too mystical and mysterious for my taste. I never understood how it looked in day-to-day practice.

But when Brenda leveled her finger at me, her words flipped the switch, and the lights came on. Sanctification simply meant to become normal, like Jesus. And to "work out" my salvation meant to stop sinning. You don't have a right to stay the same whenever you're missing His mark.

Quiz

At what baggage are those around you leveling their fingers?

Are you claiming some "right" to stay the same, or are you anxious to change…you know, to become normal, like Christ?

Has it ever occurred to you that you might not be normal?

onboard terrorist

*Be strong and of good courage, do not fear nor be afraid of them;
for the LORD your God, He is the One who goes with you. He will
not leave you nor forsake you.*

DEUTERONOMY 31:6, NKJV

I (Steve) can't imagine the guts it took for Todd Beamer and his newfound
buddies to storm the cockpit of United Airlines Flight 93 on that fateful
morning of September 11, 2001.

By now most everyone is familiar with the story of how hijackers com-
mandeered the plane—probably slitting the throat of a pilot or flight atten-
dant to show that they meant business—and directed the passengers to the
rear of the plane, where they were told not to worry, everyone was going to
be safe.

The several hijackers guarding them apparently didn't mind that some
of the passengers used their cell phones to call loved ones or, as in Todd's
case, a GTE Airfone supervisor named Lisa Jefferson. That's when these ill-
fated passengers learned that several other hijacked planes had been flown
into the World Trade Center and the Pentagon. It became obvious to Todd
that they were destined to die in a fiery crash. Something had to be done.
After reciting the Lord's Prayer with Lisa Jefferson, Todd helped organize a

strategy with three other men. "Let's roll!" he said, and the group stormed the cockpit.

In the ensuing life-and-death tussle, the plane nosedived into a Pennsylvania field, instantly killing everyone on board but sparing the lives of hundreds or thousands of others in Washington, D.C. The hijackers could have flown the doomed jet into the White House, the Capitol, or some other symbol of our free land. The courage of those men changed the course of history and today inspires us to do the right thing even in the face of terror.

Not unlike Flight 93, every man has a lurking terrorist on board his flight through life. That terrorist is Satan himself, who wants nothing more than to hijack our will and watch us crash and burn, destroying the hope and potential that God has given every man. This master terrorist escorts us to the back of the plane and says, *Don't worry—everything's going to be okay.* He directs us to stay seated, keep our seat belts fastened, and do nothing to make a difference. He hands us pornographic magazines and plays sexy videos on the television screen. He hooks you up to the Internet and says online chat rooms are great because it's only fantasy. He says it's okay to have an affair with one of the flight attendants because your wife isn't as interested in sex as you are.

Sooner or later we have to muster the courage to storm Satan's strongholds and wrest back the controls, stopping the destruction Satan has planned for us. Every man must "roll" to the front of the plane to live in the total freedom Christ provided, taking back control of the flight plan.

Traveling freedom can be dangerous in our society. Whatever you want is out there. If you like watching interesting people having sex, then rent an R-rated movie that bills itself as "sexy" and "erotic" on the video jacket. If you like listening to others talk and joke about sex, you can find those types of shows on television. If you prefer "studying" pictures of naked women, they're easily available at the convenience store or just a click or two away on the Internet.

The master terrorist has filled our world with provocative advertisements, television with nudity and immorality, movies with the most explicit sex scenes possible, and an Internet that provides instant access to thousands of pornographic sites from around the world. Those preferring something not too blatant can fantasize by thumbing through *Sports Illustrated*'s swimsuit edition, Victoria's Secret catalogs, or the bra-and-panty ads found in today's newspapers.

Satan is doing his best to convince us that this stuff is just part of being a man—that looking is normal, healthy, and safe. But letting your eyes feast on that stuff is *not* safe—nor is it right. Sure, it may *feel* right, but therein lies the foundation of a problem that goes far beyond pornography, lust, or sexual addiction. The problem begins when feelings rather than truth and God's purposes become the foundation of our actions. Once the moral compass is set on how you feel and what feels good, you trap yourself into a world where truth is no longer relevant because truth doesn't always feel good.

And we need the truth to be relevant, because truth is the only thing that preserves us and the society we live in. Trouble is, as Christians we have become so concerned about our relevance to the world that we've often become irrelevant for our day and time.

For instance, one pastor recently attended a seminar suggesting that he use movie illustrations in his sermons to be more relevant to his congregation. So he used movie illustrations from *Die Hard, Runaway Bride,* and *Titanic* in a sermon in an attempt to stay on the cutting edge of "best-practices" Christianity.

What's wrong with using movie illustrations? Nothing, per se. But all three of these movies have more than a hint of sexual immorality in them, and not one of them could be shown in heaven. Yet the pastor said nothing about that, and in doing so, he gave tacit approval to his listeners to watch these movies.

How do I know? Two nights later one of the deacons of his church was overheard at a dinner party proclaiming, "I'm so glad that our pastor has started using movie illustrations in his sermons. Now I don't have to feel guilty watching them all the time." Others were nodding their heads in agreement.

This kind of preaching and teaching does not make us relevant. It makes us irrelevant to the greatest issue of our day. These are the most pornographic days of world history, and these days are a lot like the days of Ezekiel:

> Her priests do violence to my law and profane my holy things; they
> do not distinguish between the holy and the common; they teach
> that there is no difference between the unclean and the clean.
> (Ezekiel 22:26)

Today the sexual lines have been so blurred that no one knows what's right or wrong, holy or profane. Yet we are trying so hard to be relevant that we are obscuring the truth. The truth is this: Men draw sexual gratification through their eyes. The truth is this: Men rarely get control of their sexuality until they cut off the sensual imagery in movies and the world around them. To put it bluntly, we're living in the era of masturbation.

There's more masturbation today and more things to masturbate over than ever before. There are entire industries centered on masturbation. The porn industry wants you to masturbate compulsively so it can sell you more products. *Playboy* succeeds because guys want to look at pictures of naked women and masturbate. *Playboy* has always been about masturbation, though the publisher will never say it out loud. The porn industry releases eleven thousand new "adult" movies each year so men can become aroused and masturbate in the privacy of their homes.

Porn-related Web sites are also an amazing success. Even while the dot-com industry was in a shambles, with all sorts of Internet sites going out of business, seventy thousand adult pay-for-porn sites were flourishing. Clearly, men want to masturbate, so businesses have sprung up to meet that need. And all these folks want you as a customer.

These are special days—a time when the idea of sexual purity seems radical. The good news is that God is looking for special people in these special times. His eyes are looking throughout the whole earth for men on whose behalf He can show His power—just as He did in the days of wicked king Ahab. When He needed someone with a steel spine to stand up to the evil man, God found that man in Elijah.

He's looking for men with guts like Todd Beamer, who wasn't afraid to act courageously. He's looking for Sunday-school teachers and pastors who will, with spines of steel, draw their flocks away from this world's sensuality.

But what if we seem irrelevant to them? Why not consider a far more frightening question… What if we *are* irrelevant? In our rush to seem relevant, what if we lose our saltiness as Christians and lose our purifying effect on our culture? That is true irrelevance.

If you're living on the other side in sexual purity, *being* irrelevant will terrify you far more than *seeming* irrelevant. God's standard of holiness is clear: "But among you there must not be even a hint of sexual immorality, or of any kind of impurity, or of greed, because these are improper for God's holy people" (Ephesians 5:3). This is a high standard for God's man, but it's the only one that leads to a flight through life in total freedom. I hope you're up to every man's challenge.

Quiz

Have you snarled "Let's roll" and moved to wrest control of the cockpit again?

How far are you willing to go to separate yourself to be with God and to become truly relevant in this world?

choosing obedience and transformation

You are a warrior of the living God. While you didn't always feel like a warrior before you fought your battle for sexual purity, you are one. And now that you are living on this side of the battle, you can see it more clearly than ever before.

You've fought fiercely on two fronts—the spiritual front and the physical, fleshly front—and you've proven your mettle in both. Your Father could have vaporized your lusts with a snap of His fingers, but He sent you to both fronts to fight for the cause of Christ and to test your love for Him.

Of course this test revealed nothing to God. He's known what you are made of since the dawn of time—dust. But He also knows that He's deposited a new life in you and sent the Comforter to walk at your side. He's always known what you can do in Him. He simply needs *you* to know what you can do in Him. You need that too, because sexual sin once robbed your heart of something very precious.

Every little boy sees the fight for right and desires to be an agent of good, to be the good guy who saves the day. Every little boy has dreams and visions of one day being someone great and doing something great, but sexual sin often steals these dreams away until heaven intervenes and recaptures them for God's man on the battlefield. Victory restores these hopes and renews the dreams that were once vaporized in the midst of sexual sin.

The dream lives! Now you *know* what you can do in Him. You feel it. You're a fighting machine, confident as you approach any battle. You've proven that your Commanding Officer can trust you with much as long as you abide in Him. And He's proven that you can trust Him to supply all you need in any battle.

Battles test and transform soldiers, and this test revealed the depth of your love for Him. You're stronger, and you're changed. God is a strong God, and He wants strong, confident soldiers in His kingdom who are good in a fight, even when facing daunting odds that seem overwhelming (like the tall odds you sensed as you approached your battle with sexual sin).

You also needed this test to discover the limits of Satan's power and to find that his temptations can fade in your life. The choking chains of sexual sin taught you to believe that Satan had your number and that you would always be helpless before his onslaughts, but now you know that you can hold your own through God's grace and the working of the Holy Spirit in you. You can grow, and power can flow. Yes, even in you.

Sexual sin may have once stunted your Christian growth and sapped the power of the Spirit in your life, but not anymore. Now you are ready to soar in the power of the Spirit. Every little boy dreams of flight, to rise high above the earth and to be carried by fresh winds to new heights, gazing upon thrilling vistas while far above the fray. It is lovely to be holy!

Jesus came to impart the Spirit of holiness in you, and as you are transformed and as you lose your heart and desires to Jesus, you can stretch the limits of sin's gravitational pull and soar into that sunshine of freedom. As the Holy Spirit takes the Word and makes it powerful in you, everything that presents itself against the obedience and fullness of Christ withers in its light.

the spiritual front
and the fleshly front

Flee from sexual immorality. All other sins a man commits are outside his body, but he who sins sexually sins against his own body.

1 Corinthians 6:18

Not only was I sexually promiscuous in college, I also developed a drinking problem. Alcohol loosened me up socially, which in turn loosened me up with the women (and vice versa, if they were drinking). I kept on drinking after taking my first job. I tempered my drinking because I didn't want hangovers to affect my work performance, but I still imbibed too much and too often. In the midst of this turmoil, I heard the Lord knocking on my heart's door, and I opened it to Him.

Within a few weeks I moved from the San Francisco Bay Area back home to Iowa. I didn't get into the *Cheers*-type bar scene—where everyone knows your name—so things were looking up. I *liked* working hard at my new career, pouring in seventy hours over six days of every week. Sundays were my reward, and I always spent them the same way. I'd go to church in the morning and then come back to my apartment. Then I'd open the freezer and pull out a Tony's frozen cheese pizza and lay it on a cookie sheet. I'd reach for a bag of Green Giant frozen peas and layer those beautiful green babies over the pizza. I'd sprinkle a layer of fresh mozzarella cheese on top, and *voila!* I had myself a tasty double-cheese-and-peas pizza. What could be better?

Thirty minutes later I'd sit down in front of the television with my pizza on my lap and my beloved Pittsburgh Steelers on the tube. The view from my overstuffed lounger was tremendous, as was the ice-cold bottle of Henry Weinhard beer that I clutched in my right hand. What a great reward after a hard week of work.

But one Sunday as the Steel Curtain thrashed yet another rival in the black-and-blue AFC North, God spoke a single sentence into my heart regarding the bottle in my right hand: *Why do you need that?*

While the Lord spoke just one sentence, I understood the rest of God's meaning: *Your alcohol is coming between us, and it will trip up your walk with Me because of the sexual sin it fosters.*

The football game suddenly became just background noise as I stared long and hard at that Henry's label, counting the cost. Five minutes later I stood up, walked to the sink, and poured the beer down the drain. I haven't touched a drop of alcohol since that day.

Is it a sin to drink? No. While Paul states that it is a sin to drink to dissipation or drunkenness (see Galatians 5:21), the Bible is full of references to people drinking wine, even Jesus Himself (see Matthew 11:16-19). I merely bring up this story to point out an important contrast. We often think of drunkenness as a sin against the body.

But interestingly, in 1 Corinthians 6:18, Paul leaves drunkenness among the sins committed *outside* the body, naming sexual sin as the only member of sin's "against the body" club. Why? We can look at another story to catch the difference.

After I spoke in Long Island, New York, one night, Tim cornered me and said, "I'm thankful for your practical message tonight. My story really backs you up."

"I'd love to hear about it," I said, intrigued.

"Though I have a wonderful wife who really takes care of me in bed, I've always had eyes for women and Internet porn, which led to a problem with masturbation for years. I cried and prayed long and hard for God to deliver me. One night as I slept, I believe He did."

"Really?"

"Yes, really. I had a dream where I was standing cold and lonely in a vast dark room, frightened and unable to get out. Suddenly a spotlight showed straight down on me from above, and a pure, white raiment floated down and settled over me, covering me in His grace.

"The next day I noticed that the pull toward porn had vanished. The desire was simply gone. I praised God all day, and I continued praising Him as the days and weeks passed without making any late-night visits to the computer."

"Wow, that's great!" I exclaimed. "What a story!"

"Oh, but wait. Unfortunately and sadly, that's not the end of my story. While God had delivered me miraculously, I never really dealt with my character or my looking-around habits. Last summer I was still staring long at the babes walking by with their breasts half hanging out. Before long, one girl with particularly large breasts got me pretty excited, which tripped a memory of someone who looked exactly like her at some porn site on the Internet. The next time I got online, I thought, *It wouldn't hurt to take a quick peek. I'm delivered, after all. It can't hurt me.*

I knew what was coming.

"Well, that one look led to many more over the next few weeks, and today I'm as stuck as I ever was."

Let's look a little deeper at this. While both alcohol abuse and sexual sin are against the body in one sense, you can walk away from a beer or pour it down the sink, like I did. Not so with the eyes or mind, which you can't walk away from.

Their ability to perform foreplay, to get your mind thinking of specific sex acts, is inside you and never very far away. That's why this sin is in its own special category, and that's why Paul gives us a unique prescription for handling this sin—fleeing. This tactic is critical. You either train your eyes to flee, or you just keep losing. That's just the way it is.

This is probably why many men tell me, "When I got saved, every other vice simply fell away, but my sexual sin just hangs on and on."

And as we've seen from Tim's story, even if God *does* miraculously free you in a moment of time, if you don't learn to flee, you can fall right back into your addiction. Your eyes, like a broken sewage pipe, will continue to carry in sewage and leak it into your life.

That is why we not only need to fight on the spiritual front by praying as Tim did, but we also have to fight on the physical front with our will by fleeing as Paul taught.

What does fleeing look like in practice? Simple: It is cutting off those sensual images that create that mental pop! Bouncing the eyes is one form of fleeing. Starving the mind of new images and taking lustful thoughts captive are two others. Fleeing into a deeper relationship with God through regularly reading the Bible is a fourth.

One reader came to this truth, saying, "I can finally see the practical truth you expressed in *Every Man's Battle.* For some reason my pride would not allow me to see the common sense in there until now. It's just like the Israelites were supposed to do to the Amalekites. When God told Saul to destroy them all, Saul didn't. He kept some of them alive. Later, the ones he didn't destroy came back and attacked Israel again. And I have come to the point in my life where I realize that I must hack to death all avenues of the flesh."

Jesus declared that the truth will set us free, and we can all live freely if we'd only walk in it. Granted, I may not be free to stare at or watch anything I'd like, but since I've learned to flee, I've never been freer in my life, freer to relate openly to women, freer to pray to my Lord, and freer to love my wife and to look deeply into her eyes without the guilt of my secret sin.

Quiz

Have you declared war on both fronts of the battle
    for sexual purity?
Have you won on both fronts?
Are you merely hearing the truth, or are you walking in it?

go ahead and knock it off

Come near to God and he will come near to you. Wash your
hands, you sinners, and purify your hearts, you double-minded.

JAMES 4:8

We heard from a fellow named Peter who had an interesting problem. A pastor at his church asked him if he would speak to the men's group about moral purity. Peter had had a problem with masturbation, but after reading *Every Man's Battle,* he had cut *way* back on that practice, and word got around in his accountability group. The pastor thought it would be good for the men's group to hear from someone experiencing victory on the front lines.

Peter mentioned to the pastor that *Every Man's Battle* was the reason he was no longer a slave to masturbation.

"Really," the pastor said. "In Galatians, we are told that if we walk by the spirit, we will overcome the flesh." The pastor was suggesting that we don't need books or to join any Twelve-Step program; God alone has full responsibility for our purity.

"You have a point there," Peter conceded, "but I have to tell you that I needed more than a verse to break this addiction. That's why *Every Man's Battle* was so helpful."

Peter could tell that his pastor didn't want him telling the men's group that reading a book could be the answer. The pastor didn't want his men thinking that they could beat their sexual problems by focusing on the flesh—almost willing yourself to say no to things or images that cause a man to lust and later masturbate.

I appreciate the mind-set of Peter's pastor. Believe me, I've thought about this a lot through the years. We cannot win this battle without the Holy Spirit, and on that point I speak from personal experience.

Before Christ, I was up to my neck in pornography and sleeping with girlfriends. That lifestyle had its pleasures, I can assure you, but I went through many days frustrated by the way sex dominated my mind—while I was awake and while I was asleep! On many occasions it struck me how much time and money I was wasting on these pursuits.

I swore off casual sex many times and even prayed and asked God to be closer in my life, but those promises and thoughts never lasted long. The next night I'd be right back in bed with that French graduate student—or whoever was up for a good time. I couldn't stop doing that type of stuff until I was saved. Clearly, it was the Holy Spirit who enabled me to win this battle.

That being said, the church has a strange double standard when it comes to sexual sin. When pastors counsel thieves, they don't quote Galatians. They quote Ephesians 4:28, saying, "He who has been stealing must steal no longer."

"Do you hear that buddy? Stop stealing!"

When pastors counsel liars, they don't just say, "Let's just agree together in prayer about your lying." Sure, they pray with them, but they'll also say, "Knock off your lying, and I mean now, friend! It is killing your marriage!"

On the home front, I can assure you that when Brenda laid into me about my temper, she didn't say, "Let's just pray together about your walk in the Spirit."

Instead, she got in my face and said, "Stop screaming at me and punching holes in the wall, or else!"

That's why that pastor's advice doesn't set well with me. With most sin we tell the sinner to knock it off. But with this one we often just say, "Be encouraged! Pray! Walk in the Spirit!"

If someone is running up credit-card debt on Internet porn, I wouldn't counsel him only to keep praying about it. I would also tell him to knock it off. Ditto for someone into rampant masturbation or occasional premarital sex. I've talked to young male teens who've told me that they know sexual intercourse is wrong before marriage, but they still like to get up under a bra. They say they can't commit to not having premarital sex. They want to keep their options open in case they find themselves in a bed with a girl. These guys know what the Bible says about premarital sex. They already have the power inside to do the right thing. They just don't want to do the right thing.

The Bible says, "Be perfect...as your heavenly Father is perfect" (Matthew 5:48). This is a choice we can make. Sure, we can't do it without the Spirit of God working in our lives to give us the right desire, knowledge, and power. But we can't move forward without leaving that type of behavior in our rearview mirrors either.

But that's taking pride in the flesh! Of course we are not to take pride in our flesh. But neither are we to pretend it doesn't exist! Sure, we need to walk in the Spirit as it says in Galatians, no question. But we also need to stand up like men and crucify the fleshly sinful nature, as it also says in Galatians (5:24).

When we do so, we walk in His image. God is a strong God, and He wants us to be strong men:

> Do everything...so that you may become blameless and pure, children of God without fault in a crooked and depraved generation, in which you shine like stars in the universe as you hold out the word of life. (Philippians 2:14-16)

We don't tell people to keep drunken driving to a minimum. We don't tell men to keep rape to a minimum. So why do we tell men to keep lust and masturbation to a minimum?

In fact, lusting is a little bit like rape, because lusting grabs sexual gratification from a woman against her will. If you don't believe me, then check out what Amy wrote us:

> You can feel it when a guy is lusting after you. I can't tell you how many times I've been at work or at the mall, and I could just feel some guy's eyes crawling over me like a slimy slug. That feels so gross! That's disgusting!

And not to be outdone, my wife, Brenda, said:

> It seems to me that some men are uncontrolled perverts who don't think about anything but sex. It affects my trust in men, and I don't like it that men lustfully take advantage of women in their thoughts.

Let's treat sexual sin like every other sin. It hurts and tramples those around us, as well as changes the way we look at women.

So, let's walk in the Spirit *and* knock it off.

Quiz

On the spiritual front, are you spending more time in intimate worship, prayer, and Bible reading?

On the fleshly front, have you disciplined that double-mind and that body like a soldier at war?

7

Kevin's battle

*Therefore, since we are surrounded by such a great cloud of wit-
nesses, let us throw off everything that hinders and the sin that
so easily entangles, and let us run with perseverance the race
marked out for us.*

HEBREWS 12:1

Our choice to throw off the sin that hinders and entangles plays a role as we
work out our salvation in Christ. The Spirit works in our heart to desire a
normal walk, and then we choose to walk normally. While we can do nothing without the Spirit's work, our choices are still part of the fight. Let me
share with you an amazing e-mail from a gritty champion living on the
front lines of every man's battle.

> Before I begin this e-mail, let me say that I will probably not be
> able to type the entire thing without crying. I am still getting the
> junk out of my life, and for me it comes out from way down deep
> through tears. Having said that, let me begin.
>
> On Saturday afternoon I was feeling very weak in terms of
> my "sobriety" from sexual sin. My flesh was really fighting me. My
> roommate would be out of town Saturday night until late Sunday,
> so my flesh knew there would be ample time to attack me late

Saturday night when I was alone in my apartment with my computer.

My heart was aware of his schemes and called in reinforcements. There are four of us who started this journey for sexual purity, and we are "on call" for one another anytime any one of us feels tempted, day or night. So I did just that, calling Cooper because I thought I might be able to catch him. My two other buddies were out of town.

Cooper didn't pick up the phone, so I left a message. "Call me when you get the chance," I croaked. "I'm feeling weak." Conditions were just so ripe for me to fall. Everything was lining up against me, and I mean everything.

About a half hour later, who should call but Allison? Now, Allison is a total sweetheart, and I'd take a walk in the sunshine with Allison any day of the week. I really want to get to know her better. But she struggles with sexual stuff just as I do, so guess what? She dropped a few hints that she wouldn't mind getting together to hang out later that night!

She was totally unaware that I was struggling with my sexual stuff, of course, and I'm certain her motives on the phone were pure. But she'd caught me at a very bad time…the apartment was empty, and I knew that I just might be able to persuade her to stay over. My sexual desire was starting to win.

I had to duck away fast, so I played "dense" and faked like I didn't catch her hints. But that wasn't the end of it… I couldn't keep my mind off Allison after her call all afternoon. I was all worked up, and my mind was playing with all the possibilities. My flesh knew how easy it would be to call Allison, and he was working overtime against me. And to be honest, I knew that a night with Allison would be awesome.

But deep down, my heart knew it would not be healthy at all. So I went to my apartment and grabbed my journal and hit the local coffee shop so I could stay away from the temptation. I drank a café mocha and wrote in my journal about all that I was feeling. The first line of my journal entry was this: *I'm standing on the edge of a fall... I am 214 days "sober," and I am carelessly and selfishly staring at the face of destruction.*

I really felt that. The night was so heavy on me, you know what I mean? I went on to write: *God, are you saying to me, "Adam, the way you feel right now about Allison cannot compare to the way that you will feel if you will only do this My way?"*

I pondered that for a while. The coffee shop closed, and I walked out into the heavy night alone. I got to my apartment, and there was some struggle, but not as much as before. The *only* thing that kept me from calling Allison was this thought: *Yes, it would be awesome to spend the night with her, but I remember from my past all the guilt and shame of the morning after. Allison does not need that in her life, and neither do I.*

I did not want to hurt her or contaminate her. I also had this thought: *Do I want to get with her tonight because it's Allison, or just because she's a female who can satisfy my selfish need? If Allison knew that I was thinking like this, would she still come over?* I knew that she probably wouldn't.

I sat alone on my couch as these thoughts kept swirling, when suddenly the phone rang. It was Cooper! We immediately talked about my struggle, and when I told him about how my evening had gone, he was so pumped. Before we got off the phone, I asked him if I could pray for us. I think Cooper almost fell out of his seat because I *never* ask to pray.

I remember praying the most real and honest prayer I've ever prayed. I can't remember all of it, but I said something like this: "God, in a world so dark and lost, you want us to be men of integrity and character. God, help me to remember that the true test of char-

acter comes when we are in a deep struggle, and that our true character is revealed in what we do when we are in that struggle, whether
we fall or whether we rise above it."

Fred, it was *so* real and honest. Anyway, having said all this, I did
not fall, and my sobriety is still intact! Good stuff, huh? Thanks for
letting me share. It was truly a great victory!

What an awesome display of integrity! Kevin's battle was truly epic, and
the decisions he made were positively heroic to me. When I read his e-mail
the first time, though, my heart sank. I kept waiting for the part where he
fell into sin. But that part never came—because he didn't fall.

Even though the Enemy had set his many traps, Kevin astutely avoided
them. He called his accountability partner. He played dense when Allison
asked what he was doing that night. He stayed away from his apartment so
he could stay away from his computer. He chose to value Allison's needs
more than his own desires.

What dogged integrity! And what a dauntless, relentless pursuit of
doing the right thing! Kevin is a man of valor, choosing to face every man's
challenge head-on and to stand true.

Quiz

Does Kevin's example put you to shame as a soldier in
   Christ?
Looking onto the spiritual battlefield, would the angels
   describe you as dogged and dauntless?

heavy metal

What a sight it must have been to see David trying to walk around in two hundred pounds of armor—far more than he weighed at the time! Saul's bronze helmet and coat of mail were fit for a king, grand and gloriously burnished. But David was a young kid from humble beginnings. With great courage, the shepherd boy approached the king but refused the assistance Saul offered him. Saul wasn't sure whether David was being brave or dumb, but David knew what he was doing. He went with his strength, his best weapon—flinging stones with a slingshot. He gathered just five small stones into his tiny arsenal and, with the Israeli army standing behind him, marched out resolutely to slay his giant. Turns out, he needed just one shot.

Later on David would battle another giant—lust. This time he lost, and a man was murdered and a baby died. Why? Because that time David fought alone and with the wrong weapons.

His affair with Bathsheba happened in the springtime, when kings and their armies go off to war. David, however, stayed home alone, uninvolved and unaccountable. His eyes were free to roam, and they did just that. Looking led to lust, and lust led to adultery, and adultery led to murder. Quite a progression of destruction.

If lust is a huge giant in your life, fighting all alone may lead you down the same path of destruction taken by David. Let me suggest trying something different—use your brothers in the Lord to help you. Of course this means you'll have to humble yourself by opening up to them, but there has never been a time when that has been easier to do than today. Men all around the country are talking about the most embarrassing things, including masturbation. And because they are talking about it, they are finding victory in the battle.

But even in the company of your brothers, you'll still need to take care to choose the right weapons in the battle. This past year, I (Steve) have been traveling to college campuses to speak about *Every Man's Battle* and *Every Man, God's Man.* On one campus a speaker had come through earlier suggesting that young men should masturbate before heading out on dates with their girlfriends in order to keep their passions under control. He referred to this as "pumping up." This idea caught such fire across campus that the guys printed up bumper stickers as a reminder that said "Don't Forget to Pump Up."

Now I want to be fair here. There *is* a measure of integrity in sacrificing your sexual purity through masturbation for the sake of your girlfriend's sexual purity. But is that as far as we're called to go? And is this really the proper weapon for slaying the giant of lust?

Of course not! You can't fight fire with fire. Using one type of sexual impurity (masturbation) to fight off another (premarital sex) slays nothing. Sure, you may *manage* your giant a bit better while off on your dates, but what about the rest of your life? Giants will never fall before this weapon.

But if you go with your strength, your best weapon—God's ways—you will win. I'm reminded of another campus where students began discussion groups around *Every Young Man's Battle* and formed accountability groups so they could stand together. But they also chose the right weapons.

One group of guys developed a plan to help each one stop masturbating. Each person picked a day of the week to masturbate, and that was the only day he could do it. If you missed your day, you had to wait until the next week. Once you had developed this measure of control, you moved it up a notch and picked one day every two weeks as your day of masturbation.

As it turned out, by the time the group was ready to notch it up to once every three weeks, they all agreed that the exercise had become silly and unnecessary. Each had formed so much control over their sexuality that they no longer needed a day of masturbation.

Professors told me of young men, trapped in compulsive masturbation for years, who found complete freedom as openness and accountability robbed the habit of its power to dominate their lives. Guys who had been quite reserved came out of their shells and began to connect with others in new ways. And as word of this group's victory spread, more groups grew and more young men who had felt alienated from God began to experience a connection with Him they had never known. They were all using the right weapons, fighting the battle together and finding victory together. The word *together* is the key word. If we are vulnerable and open to taking a risk with our brothers, we are never doomed to fail or to live a life of loneliness and isolation.

Jesus wants us to take His weapons and fight shoulder to shoulder:

Be prepared. You're up against far more than you can handle on your own. Take all the help you can get, every weapon God has issued, so that when it's all over but the shouting you'll still be on your feet. Truth, righteousness, peace, faith, and salvation are more than words. Learn how to apply them. You'll need them throughout your life. God's Word is an indispensable weapon. In the same way, prayer is essential in this ongoing warfare. Pray hard and long. Pray for your brothers and sisters. Keep your eyes open. Keep each other's spirits up so that no one falls behind or drops out. (Ephesians 6:13-18, MSG)

We aren't called to manage our giants. We're called to march out resolutely and to kill them together. Choose up teams and choose your weapons well. Then go out and win.

Quiz

Have you stopped short of obedience, satisfied to simply manage some sin in your life?

Are you going with your best weapons in the battle, regardless of the cost to your image?

Are you going halfway, or are you going right to the end, radically trusting God for complete victory as David did with Goliath?

the death of temptation

And we, who with unveiled faces all reflect the Lord's glory, are being transformed into his likeness with ever-increasing glory, which comes from the Lord, who is the Spirit.

2 CORINTHIANS 3:18

Why is it that some men can only get about 80 percent of the way to freedom from sexual sin? Sam was as perplexed as anyone we've known on that score:

> It was very hard for me to read *Every Man's Battle*. Even though you outline your past sins before you found your freedom, I still feel that the standard you have attained is out of my reach. Or at least out of my immediate reach.
>
> If I were to tell you that I'm struggling to get there, I feel that you would say I lack commitment—or that I don't yet hate the sin enough. That's not true. Today my pull toward lust is much less than it was six months ago, but that noose around my throat is still there.

Do I think Sam doesn't hate the sin enough? No. We think he loves bouncing the eyes a little too much. Let us explain.

In *Every Man's Battle* we wrote of three defense perimeters that have to be set up to receive total freedom from sexual sin. But the first one, bouncing the eyes, gets nearly all the attention to the exclusion of the other two. That development doesn't surprise us.

Men who have been chained up in a sexual prison year after year wonder where the promises of God have gone. Finally, someone suggests a practical solution they can understand and get their heads around, so they grab it like a drowning man going down for the third time.

Bouncing the eyes works. This practice breaks the addictive chemical cycle that is choking you, and it's the key to your cell's prison door, no question. What many guys forget, however, is that just outside the cell door is a long corridor with another heavy steel door on the other end. To get out of the prison completely, you can't stop with just bouncing your eyes. You have to be *conformed* to act like Jesus (bouncing the eyes), but you must take one more step through that second door, which is to be *transformed* by the Word to think like Jesus. The following verse explains this well:

> Do not be conformed to this world (this age), [fashioned after and adapted to its external, superficial customs], but be transformed (changed) by the [entire] renewal of your mind [by its new ideals and its new attitude]. (Romans 12:2, AMP)

How did Jesus think? Like a servant without rights. He loved righteousness and hated wickedness (see Hebrews 1:9) for His Father's sake, and He chose to give up His rights and to become a servant that He might buy us for His Father at a price.

And now that we have been bought at a price and have become servants, too, *we* must think like Jesus. We are no longer our own, and we have no rights of our own outside of Him. We spoke about this in *Every Man's Battle,* but we would emphasize it even more today because this is the key to total freedom.

Flee from sexual immorality.... You are not your own; you were bought at a price. Therefore honor God with your body. (1 Corinthians 6:18-20)

During my battle for sexual purity, I (Fred) distilled this verse down to its core kernel, which eventually transformed my mind totally:

YOU HAVE NO RIGHT TO LOOK AT THAT OR THINK ABOUT IT.
YOU HAVEN'T THE AUTHORITY.

When your mind is truly transformed to think like this, you will experience what we call the *death of temptation.* Satan's power of temptation lies in your supposed right to make decisions regarding your behavior. If you didn't believe you had that right to choose what you look at, no tempting power could touch you.

Pop-quiz time: When an e-mail with an obviously suggestive subject line appears on your screen, what is your instant reaction?

- Do you feel an immediate pull, wondering, *Should I open this e-mail?*
- Or is it a nonevent, and with a simple click you delete the suggestive e-mail without a hint of struggle?

If you're not transformed, then you still believe you have a right to choose your behavior, which means you would ask the first question. The moment you do, you open yourself to discussing the pros and cons with yourself. But far worse, you open yourself to Satan's counsel. He would *love* to be heard on this issue.

He cajoles and lies, keeping your mind focused on the conversation so you don't notice your body slipping down the slope of lust. By the time he finishes, the only answer you're ready to hear is, "Yes, you should look at it."

Therein lies the power of temptation, but temptations lose their power when we don't go there—like asking "Should I?" or "Should I not?" questions.

But let's say you have been transformed, thinking like a servant who knows that he doesn't have the right to make that decision. What's your internal response now? It doesn't occur to you to open that e-mail. The fact that you are all His and only His is so deeply ingrained that you don't even ask the question anymore, leaving no room for pros and cons to drift deceitfully about your brain. And as for Satan, since you asked no questions, no conversation with him transpires—a conversation in which he could try to get you to change your mind.

It is in this final transformation where total freedom reigns. It is here that you go beyond the "rules," per se, and go beyond your rebellious heart. You've become a servant of righteousness rather than a slave to sin. You know your place, and you've accepted it.

You see, conforming is an act of the will regarding the choices you make in life, and that is what you do when you bounce the eyes and starve the mind. But *transformation* goes well beyond your choices because it reforms your will and your mind-set at the core. If you're never transformed, your addictions are never truly put down. Your impurity can be managed, but you need to kill it.

Remember, the old you is dead. You have given up your right to choose your way, and you have been crucified in Christ. What does being crucified in Christ look like in practice?

It goes beyond the letter of the law, beyond Satan's voice, and even beyond the delight it is to do the Lord's will. Something deeper and more profound happens when you are crucified in Christ and you know your rights. Doing His will becomes a nonevent—a no-brainer, as they say. It even goes beyond your choice. *I haven't a right.* That truth is so ingrained and your mind so transformed that the right choice is made even before the sexual issue arises. You're going to walk straight because that is the only right you have.

There are no questions because everything has been settled. You are His servant, and obedience is automatic. For total victory over sexual sin, there is no more vital issue than the issue of rights.

Some doubt us, but we're telling the truth when we say there's a step where you move from the conforming position, which takes much energy, to the transformed position, which takes little energy at all. You are His, and you have the mind of Christ.

We know what you're thinking: *What do I do about those big breasts I can't help but see. After all, they're pretty hard to miss! Do the temptations stay as strong? Is it always this tough?*

Our answer is an emphatic no. Yes, the women are still there…but they just don't tempt. You will still notice beauty, but your mind will simply stop things right there. When you're transformed, you *are* transformed!

Quiz

Has sexual obedience become automatic for you?

Is obedience your way of life in every other area, too,

   or do you chafe at the Word?

the birth of His trust

"Well done, my good servant!" his master replied. "Because you have been trustworthy in a very small matter, take charge of ten cities."

LUKE 19:17

Some believe that temptation will always be there, like a parrot sitting on your shoulder and chirping away. They cite Paul's struggles with temptation and doing things he didn't want to do. Fair enough. We agree that Satan will never stop firing his grenades of temptation.

But is it really true that the power of Satan's temptations will always stay the same? Don't we ever get to a point where fewer temptations are fired our way? Don't we ever get to a point where right choices seem automatic?

Many would say no. But we've seen Christ's beauty and majesty in our lives. In light of that, we just can't think this way and we don't think Paul meant for us to think that way either.

After all, this same Paul also said that it is for freedom that Christ set us free (see Galatians 5:1) and that through Christ's resurrection we might live a new life (see Romans 6:4). If we say that the power of Satan's temptations will never change, we are also saying that nothing really changes when the new life is placed in us. We are also calling Jesus a liar when He said that the truth would set us free. And we are saying that although Christ's victory defeats the penalty of sin for all eternity, it doesn't mean greater peace and safety here on earth. If that is all His victory is worth, big deal.

But I've found that the victory at Calvary is far bigger than that. God is strong in ways that we can never imagine, and He wants us strong as well. He wants us to see the way of escape better, which He alluded to in this scripture:

> But when you are tempted, he will also provide a way out so that
> you can stand up under it. (1 Corinthians 10:13)

He wants us to be transformed into the same image of Christ from glory to glory (see 2 Corinthians 3:18) so that we can do even greater exploits (see John 14:12). If this is so, how can we say that the power of temptation never weakens or dies? If we do, that means we're saying that our tolerance level for temptation never changes.

Come on! Do you actually think that Jesus struggled with this stuff throughout His adult life on earth? Does it make sense that the Lord, who sanctified Himself on our behalf, would leave us to struggle like this? No way, as this scripture confirms:

> And so for their sake and on their behalf I sanctify (dedicate,
> consecrate) Myself, that they also may be sanctified (dedicated,
> consecrated, made holy) in the Truth. (John 17:19, AMP)

God wants us to walk normally like Jesus. If Paul meant that we can never really walk normally again in the face of temptation, what good is Christianity? And if so, why did Peter lie and say we have been given everything we need to take part in the divine nature?

Look, I've lived freedom, and I'm living it just as Scripture promises. Sure, Satan fires his rocket-propelled grenades (RPGs) from time to time, but they explode harmlessly in the sands of the desert.

He'd love to nail me, just as he'd love to nail you. He launched a shoulder-fired RPG the very night I (Fred) signed the contract to write *Every Man's Battle.* I hadn't had a sensual dream about another woman in more than ten years, yet out of the blue, one happened. As the dream opened, I was sitting against a huge shady oak in the middle of a remote grassy meadow with a nude, full-bodied, luscious woman sitting on my lap and gazing wantonly into my eyes. Quite an opening scene.

Without a trace of mental wrestling, I simply stood up, set her on the ground, and walked calmly away. Dream over.

Satan loves to hit us at high moments like this. What did Satan want? For me to fall—by that, I mean to lust after another woman in a dream—on the very day I signed the *Every Man's Battle* contract. That way he'd get me to question my fitness to be a spokesman for this series and to minister for God in this way. Some say the power of Satan's temptations never wanes until we die, but I say my dream proves that God's victory has sapped the power of Satan's temptations in my life.

Satan also likes to hit us when God is counting on us most. I remember flying into Little Rock, Arkansas, for my first national radio broadcast. I arrived at the hotel at 4:00 p.m., and since the taping wouldn't occur until the next morning, I had a whole evening to kill on my own.

And wouldn't you know it? The moment I stepped into my hotel room, I felt the Enemy's presence. Now I've told you often that I don't look for Satan behind every rock, and I wasn't looking for him this time. I also know that this story may sound weird to you, but I sensed him, just the same.

My mind flashed back to the many years in empty hotel rooms where I would battle and fight off temptations deep into the night. Satan was trying to intimidate me again by getting me into an exhausting, faith-sapping fight that would ruin my courage for the next morning's broadcast.

But I'd been transformed. I burst out laughing, saying, "Oh, really now! I should have known you'd try something like this!"

Then, with a fierce fire that burned up from my gut, I snarled, "Now get out of here right now, in the name of Jesus. I've had it with you, and I won't have this tonight!"

In that very instant he was gone, and I didn't sense him again. I had the most peaceful night in a hotel room you could imagine, and the broadcast taping went beautifully the next morning. Some say we will always struggle hard with temptation until we're sitting in heaven, but not only has Jesus not left us to struggle, He gives us the authority to stand against temptation.

In another lonely hotel room on another night in Alton, Illinois, I was preparing for my first pastors conference. Around forty pastors and their spouses had gathered to hear me speak on sexual purity, and I was duly challenged and honored to be speaking to God's chosen servants in this way.

Satan fired a vicious RPG my way. Two hours into my night's sleep, I was awakened by sensual cryings and groanings from the next room. For more than an hour, I was treated to the passionate wailings of a woman's buildup to orgasm after orgasm. Eventually, the two lovers wore each other out, and I fell asleep, only to be awakened at dawn by another round of their passions.

Years ago I'd have succumbed easily to this temptation, going along for the ride in my fantasies. But on this night, I didn't waver and the choice was automatic. I simply clamped down on my thoughts and took every one of them captive, keeping everything in check.

While I didn't awake particularly fresh that morning, I *did* awake victorious, ready to minister to a fine group of pastors. Some say that our tolerance for temptation never changes, but I say that our tolerance level for temptation *does* change and for the better.

If we can't be transformed, and if the power of temptation never weakens or dies, how could God ever trust any of us in ministry? It is only after transformation that He can truly trust you. When I founded our church's intercession group, and it began growing in numbers and strength, I often felt amazed—and overwhelmed by it all.

Once, in my desperation and discouragement, I prayed, "Lord, why in the world did You choose me for this important position? I don't feel qualified at all!"

His answer surprised me: *If you hadn't taken care of your sexual sin, I could not have used you in this way. I wouldn't have been able to trust you with the women.*

Once He can trust you, God will give you a place of service fit for trustworthy men. Like Jabez in the Old Testament, God will see you as honorable:

Jabez was honorable above his brothers.... Jabez cried to the God of Israel, saying, Oh, that You would bless me and enlarge my border, and that Your hand might be with me, and You would keep me from evil so it might not hurt me! And God granted his request. (1 Chronicles 4:9-10, AMP)

God wants to freely bless you, and once He knows you've allowed His work to be completed in you, He also knows you're ready to run with the horses on any battlefield. He's freer to enlarge your borders and to expand your tents in His service.

What's life like on the other side of purity? You can stand like a man. There is freedom, and that's the kind of life we're meant for.

Quiz

Is the power of temptation fading in your life?
Have you allowed His transforming work to have its way
   in you?
Do you have the mind of Christ—that servant's mind-set?

a man of the Word

For the word of God is living and active. Sharper than any double-edged sword, it penetrates even to dividing soul and spirit, joints and marrow; it judges the thoughts and attitudes of the heart.

Recently, I headed south to speak about mutual submission to 163 guys at a wonderful new retreat center in northeast Oklahoma. This was the first time I was to share the message of *Every Man's Marriage* to an all-male audience, so I was pumped!

Pastor Joel was excited too. His theme for the event was "Becoming Men of Valor," and just before we started he told me, "I'm going to spill my guts this weekend, and I don't want to do it alone. After reading about the early years of your marriage, I knew you were just the man to spill his guts with me!"

On Friday night he shared a gripping personal story that he'd never talked about before in public. I sat there spellbound as he described how his four-year-old daughter was raped by a young teen while on a family trip to Disneyland. The brutal sexual attack happened in the garden area around the pool while Pastor Joel and his wife Linda were packing up to return home after their visit to the "Happiest Place on Earth."

How ironic. The young girl, barely out of her toddler years, wasn't mature enough to tell her parents what had happened. On their part, Joel and Linda had seen nothing and suspected nothing, so though their daughter was acting a bit strangely, they dismissed it. The young family simply jumped into the car right on schedule for the long drive back to Oklahoma.

But later on during the ride, their daughter began bleeding profusely, and Joel and Linda knew they had a real problem. Suspecting a severe kidney infection, they headed to the nearest emergency room when they arrived in Phoenix. Little did they know that their nightmare had just begun.

Upon examining the little girl, the doctors called the police, who immediately suspected Pastor Joel of rape and incest. They locked up Joel in another room and swept their daughter away to a safehouse. At one o'clock in the morning on New Year's Eve, the authorities told Linda that she would never see her daughter again. Then, spinning icily, they marched out of the room, leaving her to cry alone in the night.

For four interminable days Joel and Linda suffered in agony and confusion. They didn't know where their daughter had been taken, and with the Department of Human Services closed down for the holiday, they had no way of reaching anyone. Finally, on the fourth day, they got an appointment with a social-service worker.

While they racked their brains during those long days, they hadn't a clue what had happened to their daughter back in California. But God knew exactly what had happened and who had done this awful thing. In the wee hours one morning as Joel tossed in a fitful sleep, his wife sat alone sobbing and praying in the bathroom. Suddenly God broke into her thoughts and revealed exactly what happened to their daughter in the minutest detail. Scribbling it down, she awakened Joel to share it with him. God seemed so wonderful, and they were so grateful!

But now they stood before the social worker, and things didn't seem quite so wonderful. Linda was petrified to tell her that she hadn't actually seen the rape or spoken to witnesses but that she had learned the details of the attack from God during prayer. She didn't want to appear loony and do further damage to their case, but she also knew she had no choice but to tell her this truth.

So through her tears Linda shared that a twelve-year-old boy had raped her daughter in the pool's garden area and that he had threatened to drown her if she didn't let him do it. Linda continued until she had shared every detail that God had revealed to her.

As she finished her story, the social worker smiled brightly and said, "That is exactly what your daughter told us this morning. Because your story matches her story word for word, we have to release her to you."

They were reunited with their daughter on the spot, and they were soon on their way home again to Oklahoma. The young boy was never caught, however.

Joel's session held us spellbound for three hours. No one watched the clock, as if we were suspended in time. The next day my sessions were also emotionally charged, and together our stories penetrated the hearts of the men. The prayer times after each session were breathtaking.

But let's freeze the frame here and run a quick flashback. How did the retreat begin? Joel didn't start with the story of his little girl. Instead, he opened with an hour of speaking from God's Word, building the "Men of Valor" theme by quoting this passage from Nehemiah:

When Sanballat heard that we were rebuilding the wall, he became angry and was greatly incensed. He ridiculed the Jews,
and in the presence of his associates and the army of Samaria,
he said, "What are those feeble Jews doing? Will they restore their
wall? Will they offer sacrifices? Will they finish in a day? Can they
bring the stones back to life from those heaps of rubble—burned
as they are?"...

So we rebuilt the wall till all of it reached half its height, for the
people worked with all their heart.

But when Sanballat, Tobiah, the Arabs, the Ammonites and the men of Ashdod heard that the repairs to Jerusalem's walls had gone ahead and that the gaps were being closed, they were very angry. (Nehemiah 4:1-2,6-7)

Today many Christian men (perhaps you, too) come from weak family backgrounds with little Christian heritage. When you are saved, you are called to rebuild the fallen walls in your life—walls broken down by childhood pain, marital strife, current attacks of the Enemy...you name it.

Often your reconstruction project goes well at first, and while you may still have some major gaps in your walls, you feel good because you know you're getting there. But the Enemy soon gets incensed. You are closing gaps in your life where he once had free access, so he brings out the big guns of intimidation, increasing the oppression in your life. "You're a feeble little man," he rages. "You're out of your league. You'll never be restored. Besides, look where you came from! Look at that big old pile of burnt rock that you call your life!"

The potshots work. "Maybe he's right," you say. "I've been working with all my heart, but the work is getting harder. This ain't fun, and we're only half done. With all this rubble, I don't know if I can make it."

You need to move higher with the Holy Spirit and become a spiritual man of valor in Him. Did you know that the name Nehemiah means "counselor," and that Nehemiah was a "type" of the Holy Spirit? In Nehemiah's day, Sanballat rose up against him, and Nehemiah challenged the people to respond, in effect saying, *Are you going to take the wall halfway, or are you going to take it up a notch?*

Today when your enemy rises up, *your* Counselor delivers a similar challenge: *You have problems. Do you want to take things to another level?* The Spirit is calling you to become a man of valor.

Pastor Joel, in dissecting the fourth chapter of Nehemiah, laid out the ten traits of a man of valor. I'll list three of them here:

- Make a good, honest inspection of your walls and acknowledge the lowest points (from verses 13 and 14).
- Stand up and remember the Lord, opening yourself wide for supernatural encounters with God (from verse 14).
- Get a fighting spirit inside of you and understand that your family is at stake (from verse 14).

Pastor Joel planted the Word deeply that Friday night, and as I said, the rest of the conference went great. I flew home Sunday afternoon utterly bushed after speaking twice during the Sunday morning services at Joel's church.

But Pastor Joel didn't leave it there. He closed the weekend at their Sunday night service by asking some men to share the retreat's impact.

Normally I don't ask for audiotapes of these interactions, but the Lord prompted me to get them. What I heard caught me totally off guard. Twelve men got up and spoke that night, but only two directly mentioned my name or my teaching sessions. *What's up with that?* I thought.

My ego wasn't hurt. I was simply perplexed. *How could this be?* After all, I was there. I saw the emotion and the prayers. *I don't get this!*

Confused, I listened to the tapes again. This time I noticed that the men didn't refer much to Joel's powerful story either. So what did these men talk about? The impact of God's Word from Joel's opening remarks. The impact of the Holy Spirit's call as He leveled Nehemiah's challenge to become men of valor.

I also noticed something else. They didn't speak only of the retreat's impact. Each man shared how the Holy Spirit had been wooing and calling them for weeks, months, and even years. While the retreat sessions brought important encounters with God, these were only links in a longer chain of encounters that they'd had with Him over time through the written and spoken Word.

Let me share what one man said, a fellow I'll call Alan, who was one of the two to refer to my talks. (I've italicized key phrases to emphasize the Spirit's work through the Word in Alan's life.)

I would have fit fine into Fred's family. We yelled about everything too, and we took great pride in that. That was normal for us.

I've rationalized this and *thought I had worked on this for years.* Then *a number of weeks ago,* something happened at home, and I blew up. I apologized immediately. "Honey, I thought I'd really made some progress with this," I said.

My wife responded, "I wish you would have asked me or asked the kids. We would have told you that isn't true!" *I felt so convicted in my spirit.* Then *about two weeks ago,* something happened, and I blew up again. *Again I was deeply convicted by the Spirit.*

A few days later, the Lord said to me, "Alan, it is written that it is not what goes into you that defiles you, but that which comes out of you that defiles you, and that which has been coming out of you has been defiling your wife and your children."

I was sick to my stomach *at His Word,* and my heart ached. Then *the evangelist came last weekend, and I heard the Lord say,* "You take great joy in hearing the Word and in seeking the truth, and you take great joy in the fact that you love Me so much that I can never shake you off. *But what will you do with this word I'm sharing* about your anger?"

Then *the Holy Spirit spoke this scripture to me:* "Husbands, love your wives, just as Christ loved the church and gave himself up for her" [Ephesians 5:25]. Then He said, "Submitting to My truth about your anger is your act of giving up your self for your wife. *Do this as unto the Lord.*"

Then came the retreat. Fred didn't call it "defiling our wives."

He called it "trampling." When he said that, in my mind I saw Wile E. Coyote getting squished by the big boulder that fell on him. "I've been doing that to my wife? I've been doing that to my kids?"

I thought back to Friday night when Pastor Joel *talked about Nehemiah.* He told us, "The first step in being a man of valor is *to make a good inspection and to acknowledge what you've done.* Another step is *to get a fighting spirit.* Do you smell the battle, guys? Men of valor love the smell of battle and run to the battle!"

Well, I do smell it, and I've finally realized that my family is at stake! I'm running to the battle, and *I'm going for the truth.*

Hmmm. I began to realize something clearly after hearing twelve of these. Pastor Joel is one of the greatest pastors I've known, but he was not the main event. All he really was on Friday night was just another friend sharing a story about God's amazing grace in his family's life and encouraging these guys to look up and answer the call.

And me? I was just another friend sharing my story of His amazing grace and encouraging them to see that Christ can do anything in us.

But it was Jesus they couldn't stop talking about, and it was His Word that had their hearts racing. Jesus was more than just another friend sharing stories of amazing grace. Jesus *is* the story, and He *is* amazing grace.

What's more, Jesus is the Word in flesh. Do you know what that means? An encounter with Scripture is, in truth, an encounter with Jesus. It is a transforming encounter with God Himself.

Men of valor open themselves wide for encounters with God and His Word. That's exactly what these guys needed and exactly what they sought. Sure, they loved Pastor Joel, and many said they'd been looking forward to hearing me speak at the retreat.

But an encounter with us means nothing unless it leads to an encounter with God and His Word, who causes everything to grow:

I planted the seed, Apollos watered it, but God made it grow. So neither he who plants nor he who waters is anything, but only God, who makes things grow. (1 Corinthians 3:6-7)

Ah, yes. Like Paul, Pastor Joel planted the seed of God's Word on Friday night. We both watered that seed with our own stories. But God made it grow, so God got the increase, and God was all they could see.

And now I could see. Like Apollos, I was simply God's water boy. As I recognized this, a deep satisfaction settled over my soul. I liked being God's water boy. The impact of His Word was complete that weekend, and now the audiotapes made perfect sense.

What about you? When was the last time you heard a fresh word from God, either through prayer's revelation or through the written Word leaping to life before you in the Spirit?

Are you allowing God's Word to have its impact in you? Are you hungry for that encounter, or are you holding back in the rear of the congregation, marking time? Get hungry for God! You must be a man of the Word, and you must change the way you view Scripture—an encounter with the Word is an encounter with God.

What's keeping you from kicking it up a notch and becoming a spiritual man of valor? Men of valor run to the smell of battle. "Remember the Lord, who is great and awesome" (Nehemiah 4:14). Seek Him through His Word, and He will transform you completely.

Quiz

Are you steadfastly seeking regular encounters through the written Word?

Are you listening intently to the Spirit's spoken Word as you run to battle?

he obeyed

It was by faith that Noah built an ark to save his family from the flood. He obeyed God, who warned him about something that had never happened before.

HEBREWS 11:7, NLT

Noah was a man of great faith, character, and obedience. Here was a man who stood so far out in a crowd of sinners that God spared his life and the lives of his family when the rest of the world was destroyed by the Flood. Noah's story is courageous and bold, and not just because he was the captain of the largest floating zoo in history.

Think back to what it must have been like to be building a *huge* boat in the middle of a hot desert while the rest of the world played on. Matthew 24:38 tells us, "In those days before the Flood, the people were enjoying banquets and parties and weddings right up to the time Noah entered his boat" (NLT). The last thing the party animals of the day imagined was that the entire land would be flooded.

What Noah and his boys were doing made no sense, and the locals must have thought these guys were crazy. Noah was building the largest ship they had ever seen on land far from any body of water that could possibly float that boat. And this flood business? Come on!

Yet year after year Noah and his family labored on, toiling 36,000 days at the family boat factory. Every single day must have taken a grand act of faith to continue. I (Steve) think that on day 34,987, I might have been a little weary of the process and inclined to abandon ship.

How huge was this boat? Scripture tells us Noah's ark was 450 feet long, 75 feet wide, 45 feet high with three decks to carry two of each living creature on the earth. Since Noah's boys were real people, I have wondered if Ham or Shem carved clever things into the side of the ark, like "My Other Boat Is a Dinghy" or "Got Umbrella?" Whatever finishing touches they might have put on the ark, we know they finished it right on time. As they completed the "load in" of the world's largest zoo, a few raindrops fell from the sky, and they quickly buttoned things up for what was to come. Noah obeyed God in the most trying of circumstances, and Scripture records his obedience several times in the Old and New Testaments.

Most everyone is aware that the Bible is divided into these two parts, and each testament is full of God's truth and amazing stories, some of victory and some of defeat. We can all see our lives mirrored in these real-life stories that present the strengths and weaknesses of all God's children.

Fast-forward two thousand years from today. Let's assume that for some reason a third testament of the Bible is written, called the Newest Testament. In the Newest Testament, you'll once again be reading stories of God's people. Now imagine that somehow, some way, your story made it into the third testament of the Bible.

What would it say?

Would your story honor your family for generations to come, or would it be a source of embarrassment and shame? What is the lesson that could be learned from your life when people read it two thousand years from now? What will history record about you?

I don't know of anyone whose story could top Noah's. In Genesis 6:22, we read, "Noah did everything exactly as God had commanded him" (NLT). Wow! It doesn't get much better than that—a bar set on the highest slot on the two poles.

I (Steve) didn't always set the bar too high. In the Newest Testament my early story would have to be recorded along these lines: "He did everything exactly as God commanded him half the time, every now and then, whenever it suited him, or sometimes when it was easy." Earlier parts of my story would be even worse: "He only obeyed his appetites and his urges for instant gratification." How sad.

I don't think that future testament will ever be written, of course, but today there is a page being written in a different book—the Book of Life. God, in a way only He understands, is recording the events and decisions that we make every day. Today and every day we have an opportunity for these entries to glorify God and further His kingdom.

You know, we won't be asked to build a huge ark in the middle of the Mojave Desert, but each of us has already been asked to obey God all of the time, like Noah. At the end of *this* day, a two-word entry in His hand ought to be recorded in the Book of Life: "He obeyed."

Quiz

What is your legacy of obedience? Is it crystal clear?

a fresh view of sin

Have you ever heard a pastor or speaker say, "Don't sin!"

You probably have. What emotion does this phrase conjure up in you? For many, I would venture that hearing someone say "Don't sin!" resurrects feelings of a negative, fearful view of sin. In fact, we run from calling sin, sin these days because we're afraid it will hurt our relationships with others and will dry up and diminish a rich, emotional relationship with God. Nothing could be further from the truth. Calling sin, sin is not narrow, and a clear focus on sin should not wreck relationships…it should fertilize them and release them to grow.

We need a fresher view of sin. It even might be helpful to have a whole new word for *sin*. God's laws are good, and they are meant to be our friends. His laws teach us what is normal and what is not, yet we fixate too much on the restrictions represented by the word *sin*.

It's not that the word *sin* is a poor one. The literal Greek meaning— "missing God's mark"—is right on target. Even that emotional impact that the word *sin* evokes shouldn't be a problem, because we need a word that elicits urgency and respect. After all, sin is a dangerous thing. Any veteran of the battle for sexual purity knows firsthand the destruction, bondage, and spiritual disease that sin carries with it. We need to fear God and respect sin for our own good.

Still, a second word for *sin* would better capture God's heart toward our transgressions in this age of grace. Because of our forays into legalism over the past decades, however, the word *sin* fogs over the love that God passionately feels for us, the very love that prompted God to define His laws in the first place.

God is not a grump, and He is not mad all the time. Oh, He's plenty angry at Satan and the arrogant sinfulness of the lost. His wrath will be poured out one day, make no mistake. Sin is still about hell and damnation for them.

But His view toward *our* sin is quite different. We're His children, and He sees us through the redemption of Jesus Christ. Our Father might say it this way: "I've called you, and My favor is upon you. I will not forget you because you are loved and you are mine!"

For us as His children, sin shouldn't be about doing the right thing or else! That isn't why He defines His laws so clearly for us or why He cares so passionately about our holiness and obedience. After salvation, God's laws are about grace and love, not judgment. About freedom and living normally and abundantly. About our relationship with Him and our relationships with those around us. Sin obscures Christ as well as His love and truth. That's what He hates. He's not against us. He's for us, and my own life proves it.

When I was in sexual sin, I couldn't get away from God. He would whisper this verse to me day after day after day:

Why do you call me, "Lord, Lord," and do not do what I say?
(Luke 6:46)

Why do you suppose God chased me up and down the highways and byways of my early Christian life with this verse? Was He angry with me and trying to be mean? No. Was He trying to pound me into submission like some relentless interrogator? No.

He wanted me to be normal, and He wouldn't rest until I was, because He loved me so. While He challenged me with that verse hundreds of times, He never barked it at me with a harsh, judgmental edge. He simply kept the truth before me, because He knew that the truth would set me free.

And He wanted me free. He wanted my marriage free. He wanted my sons and my family tree free from generational bondage that choked it like some all-consuming, binding vine.

Today the word *sin* way too often misses this aspect of God's heart regarding the Law. When His Word says, "Avoid all sin," we miss the "I love you, my child" that lies behind it. He wants so much to have a tight relationship with us, but our sin gets in the way of our intimacy with Him.

What God hates most about sin is the effect it has on relationships. God wants all our relationships to draw others to Him. He doesn't want us to be His children in name only. He wants us to look *like* His children and to walk normally like Jesus.

In defining sin clearly, God's focus is on relationships. It is not designed to kill your fun but to define what love actually is:

> I am not writing you a new command but one we have had from
> the beginning. I ask that we love one another. And this is love: that
> we walk in obedience to his commands. (2 John 1:5-6)

The Law is all about love and relationship. What is love for your neighbor? Answer: obedience to God's commands. To God they are one and the same. In fact, we can't really be sure we're loving one another unless we're really sure what sin is. By laying out sin clearly, God simultaneously sketches out what love looks like in practice and what actions trample relationships.

Now the more I think about it, *trampling* makes a great second word for *sin* because it really captures God's focus on relationships. Trampling crushes true intimacy. Trampling is sinning against those around you.

Yes, I said *sinning.* Most of us Christian men sin against our wives regularly, but we're just too blind to see it.

Of course, it's always easier to understand trampling in reverse. If your wife cuts off sexual relations with you or only makes herself available once a month, you're feeling crushed at the center of your being. You've been trampled, and you feel small and disrespected. She may see it as an individual choice that she has a right to make, but within the context of your relationship, you've been trampled, and that's wrong.

We can also spot it from the other direction if we listen carefully to our wives. Take this e-mail, for example:

I feel weird writing this, but I am losing hope. My husband of nine years has a lust problem and openly ogles other women. He's gotten counseling twice, but he doesn't really see what is wrong with it. I brought up the subject again two months ago and told him I would no longer accept this.

I know I am not what I used to be, and I will never be what he likes. He says that there is more to loving me than just liking the way I look. I realize this, but it hurts so much when I see him giving other women second and third looks. How do I get it across to him that it is wrong for him to keep this ideal woman in his head to which I will never compare? I know this is not what God intended marriage to be, and I feel so crushed that I am finding it hard to want to stay in it.

This husband may not recognize his ogling as sin, but he ought to within the context of this relationship. His wife's trampled heart lies bare before him every day.

We often run from calling sin, sin these days, but to keep from trampling our relationships, we need a clearer, broader view of sin, not a narrower one. Your view of sin is too narrow if you only see things from your own point of view, because as you can see from the two examples above, depending solely on your own point of view doesn't reach far enough. Things that may not look like sin to you on the surface may clearly be sin within the context of your relationships. Sin tramples, and the trampling in these stories is obvious.

Gratefully, your battle for sexual purity has given you a fresher view of sin, broadening your understanding of how sin ruins the pictures painted by your relationships. And while the word *sin* may have grated on you at one time because of its restrictions, you're beginning to see that God's call to holiness is less about toeing lines than it is about eradicating land mines in your relationships with man and God.

Where the word *sin* once sparked rebellion in you, it should now spark a deeper desire to paint lovely pictures for Him in your relationships, pictures free of sin's trampling destruction.

calling sin, sin

*You have loved righteousness and hated wickedness; therefore
God, your God, has set you above your companions by anointing
you with the oil of joy.*

Hebrews 1:9

What if we don't call sin, sin? Brenda and I recently counseled Megan and
Gary through a marital crisis. Megan had tired of their marriage and had
stepped into an affair. In frustration and confusion Gary exclaimed, "How
do you justify this? Aren't you a Christian?"

"Yes!" Megan replied in a huff.

"Then how do you justify this?"

"There you go again, judging me!" Megan protested.

"I'm not judging you. This is black-and-white stuff from the Bible!
Besides, there isn't another culture in the world where it's okay for a wife to
have sex with another man. It isn't right by any standard!"

Cornered, Megan blurted, "Why can't you do what you want to do,
and I'll do what I want to do?"

This was bizarre to me. How could a professing Christian ask this last
question? I've seen too many folks call themselves Christians over the years
but then do whatever they wanted. They refused to accept that their sinful

behavior was, well, a sin. And when any of us refuses to call sin a sin, we paint a confusing picture to everyone around us. *Are you a Christian or aren't you? Who can tell?*

The early apostles—Peter, Paul, and John—all said salvation should have the same effect on every believer—it should give him or her a love for righteousness. Paul insisted that a profession of Christ must be accompanied by a conscious rejection of ungodliness and a choice of godly living:

For the grace of God that brings salvation has appeared to all men.

It teaches us to say "No" to ungodliness and worldly passions, and

to live self-controlled, upright and godly lives in this present age.

(Titus 2:11-12)

When we bear Christ's name but are negligent in bearing Christ's image, we sin. We are mixing God's standards with our emotions and with the sophisticated standards of the world.

People buy into sophistication all the time without thinking. Dr. Willard F. Harley, the author of the fine book *His Needs, Her Needs,* doesn't buy into this sophistication, but he saw an example of it the time he went on *The Sally Jesse Raphael Show.*

"When I arrived, I noticed the room was full of women," Dr. Harley said. "Every cameraperson was a woman. The producers were women. The audience was women, and the other guests were women. I was the only man in sight.

"The topic was infidelity, and the two women guests took the position that infidelity had its place, and that in certain situations infidelity was okay. [This is what we mean by the sophisticated view, often not questioned.] I took the position that infidelity was like a heroin addiction and that infidelity destroyed people, like the betrayed spouse. It destroyed the children. It destroyed the extended family. But it also destroyed the person engaged in the infidelity and the lover. Everyone in sight is destroyed. I said that if you can do something to preserve faithfulness in your marriage, you will avoid making a huge mistake in life. I got a standing ovation from the audience. Sally Jesse Raphael said, 'If I had read this book, my life would have been very different and very much improved.'"

Dr. Harley is to be commended for turning around an audience that shrugged off marital infidelity, but in too many quarters these days, infidelity is looked at as no big deal, and the same with divorce. Both are accepted, even in the church. We think, *Well, divorce is okay, and in some cases, it can even be good!*

But that's not how God thinks. God hates divorce (see Malachi 2:16). Jesus said it was never God's intention to allow divorce, and the only reason people do it is because their hearts are hard (see Matthew 19:8-9). It's not because we *can't* love our spouses, it's because we *won't* love them.

Look, I understand divorce, and I wouldn't think of pointing fingers. My mom was divorced three times, and my dad, twice. I've seen it all, up close. Nor am I judging my mom because she dumped three husbands: One was a wife-beater, one was an alcoholic, and another was a serial adulterer (my father).

I myself was near divorce in my own marriage because of my hard heart, but that's exactly my point. Hard hearts were at the center of all of these situations, just as Jesus said would happen. We must see things as Jesus sees them.

Can you really paint a true picture of God if you don't maintain a biblically sound view of infidelity and divorce? Have you hated wickedness and loved righteousness? If so, then you must call sin, sin, as Jesus does.

You must call it sin in order to have the proper urgency about it and to stay free. You have to recognize it for what it is—a bear trap capable of crushing you and trampling your family and your friends. Sin affects your relationship with God and your relationships with others, so you have to call it what it is. How else can you walk normally in the midst of your relationships? Consider this letter from a reader:

A few months ago my wife told me that she was considering a divorce because I hadn't given her enough intimacy over the course of our nine-year marriage. Then she told me she'd been having an online affair with an old boyfriend. She said she did this because she felt neglected by me.

Every Man's Marriage opened my eyes to how God wanted me to treat my wife. After recommitting myself to God, I underwent extraordinary changes for the better, and my outlook on life and my marriage began to improve. I now have an unconditional love for my wife, and I have forgiven her for this affair, partly because I know I'm to blame. Because of these changes, my wife now sees me in a different light, and she says that I have become the man she has always wanted. We have actually become close and even intimate again.

Just one little problem has cropped up. Well, it's a big problem: My wife will not let go of the other man because she thinks that rediscovering her love for him may have been meant to be. While she sees what I have become now, and she *does* find hope for us in that, she sees *more* promise of finding happiness with him because, while it took her almost ten years to get intimacy out of me, it came from him easily and freely after only a few short months. As you can imagine, she's become confused and torn by the decision she must make.

My wife considers herself a Christian and says that she has a strong personal relationship with God. She says she is praying for wisdom. But she also told me that she prayed earlier and asked God whether she should allow the affair to happen. She said that since she felt no regrets or guilt as the affair unfolded, she felt God was telling her that it was right thing to do.

This is where touchy-feely Christianity gets you into trouble and why abundant life never comes. Calling sin, sin—and having an affair *is* sin— would fix that and destroy this confusion, bringing real freedom.

For instance, if she called sin, sin, she wouldn't be confused into thinking that her affair was "meant to be." She would *know* that it was never meant to be, because God *always* hates infidelity.

She wouldn't be confused into thinking there's more promise in this affair than there is in the marriage. God always loves to reclaim, renew, and restore a marriage tottering on divorce, and He will always put His full attention and power into such marriages. What's more promising than that?

Finally, she wouldn't be confused into thinking she needs to pray about this. The answers are already settled in Scripture. God could not have answered that her original affair was the right thing because He hates infidelity…it is always sin. If she prays now and hears any other answer besides *Avoid divorce at all costs,* she is not hearing from God. Instead, she is hearing from her emotions or, even worse, from the Enemy, who despises marriage and wants to destroy hers.

And trust us, her marriage will be destroyed if she continues down the path of adultery with the other man. If there's any praying to be done, it ought to be a prayer of repentance and a full commitment to God's ways.

Quiz

Do you and God call the same things sin?
Does the word *sin* bug you?

calling faux, faux

In those days there was no king in Israel; everyone did what was right in his own eyes.

JUDGES 21:25, NASB

Did you grow up in a legalistic home? I'm talking about being raised by parents who banned dancing, bowling alleys, roller-skating, playing cards, and going to the movies. My friend Ed said, "When I was growing up, there were fifteen thousand no's for every three yeses. I didn't want my kids to hear a bunch of no's all the time."

That's understandable—even commendable—since intimacy with God can't be attained by merely following a bunch of man-made rules. Today the pendulum is swinging the other way, toward a more experiential, relational focus to our faith. But sometimes I wonder if it's swinging too far. What I mean is that some of us Christians are so ignorant of right and wrong that we don't even know when we are sinning.

Let me give you an example. A local youth group divides into small groups led by lay leaders on Sunday nights for relationship building and fun. Tanner, one such lay leader, recently called the parents to let them know he was going to be showing a PG-13 movie. He wanted to make sure that was okay with them. But when one parent objected to the movie, Tanner's response at the next leaders' meeting was to scornfully sniff, "Parents who don't let their kids watch movies like this are *so* anal!" Laughter ensued.

I was not at the meeting, and Tanner was directing that comment primarily at the parent involved, but when I heard about it, I was hurt and offended because he was calling my convictions anal too. The apostle Paul criticized such comments as sin because they rupture unity:

> Why do you criticize and pass judgment on your brother? Or you,
> why do you look down upon or despise your brother? For we shall all
> stand before the judgment seat of God. (Romans 14:10, AMP)

But Tanner didn't even know he was sinning. Tanner is a hip, popular guy who thinks he's got it all together as a Christian. But when I asked one of Jasen's friends from that youth group what he thought of Tanner as a youth leader, he replied matter-of-factly, "He's really friendly and fun to be around, but you wouldn't want him to be your spiritual leader."

Yet too often that is exactly the kind of spiritual leader we are choosing these days. We aren't looking for those who have proven they are walking normally, like Christ. We're looking for those who are friendly and fun to have around, guys who can get relationships growing and give the "experience" of church a little more "life."

One church recently selected such a leader for their young couples group. Tony sometimes travels on three-day weekends, and when he does, he drops by Circuit City and purchases a combination television/video player for his car. After using it on his trip, he simply returns it to Circuit City the following Monday and tells them he's changed his mind about his purchase. He sees nothing wrong with that, and most of the class laughs when he tells them how he beats the system with Circuit City.

What good are warm, friendly churches if we're behaving just like everyone else in the world, doing whatever is right in our own eyes? Is that really spiritual? As long as we're friendly and our worship team is hot, we think our Christianity is really smoking. But I gotta tell you, that's faux Christianity, as apostate as the Israelites ever dreamed of being.

You see, we may be connecting with one another, but we aren't really loving one another. Loving requires an obedience to God's commands:

This is how we know that we love the children of God: by…carrying out his commands. (1 John 5:2)

Being a "people person" doesn't make a leader. Tanner wasn't loving me, because he broke God's command by mocking the personal convictions of parents like me. Tony wasn't loving his students, because he wasn't obeying God's commands about honesty. And he wasn't teaching them how to live normally, like Jesus. Tanner and Tony were sinning, and sin tramples unity. While they're friendly enough and popular, the relationships they spawn through their leadership will remain shallow and weak.

When we jettison the Law in favor of the experience, we're not loving the lost, either. We don't realize that our slack standards are costing us in our witness to the world. In *Revival Praying*, Leonard Ravenhill writes:

This present day is like an arena whose terraces are filled with the militant godless, the brilliant and belligerent skeptics, plus the blank-faced heathen millions, all looking into the empty ring to see what the Church of the living God can do. How I burn at this point! What are we Christians doing?

I think we're enjoying ourselves and looking for the next experience, which is no different from what everyone else outside the church is doing. And this is why we have so little to offer the lost. Sadder still, we've got little to offer God.

The Law never was about guilt and shame. God doesn't just hate sin because it offends Him and He's a grouch. The main reason He hates sin is because of what it does to relationships. The Law was always about relationships, and not just about relationships with one another. It was also about our relationship with God.

How do we know we love God? Again, the apostle John was never clearer:

This is love for God: to obey his commands. (1 John 5:3)

As we've raced from our legalistic ways, we've dumped the Law and lost a proper focus on sin. While we might be longing to connect with Him and to experience Him, we can't really know Him without knowing the Word, and we can't really love Him without keeping His commands:

Whoever has my commands and obeys them, he is the one who loves me. He who loves me will be loved by my Father, and I too will love him and show myself to him. (John 14:21)

To keep His commands, we must know His commands. The Law, too, is spiritual (see Romans 7:14), and if *we* want to be spiritual, we must be willing to view sin as broadly and clearly as He does.

Loving God and others isn't only an emotion. It is also an action, and anything less is not fully spiritual. We've said we must be willing to call sin, sin. We must also be willing to call faux, faux.

Quiz

Has "walking in love" and "walking in obedience" become totally synonymous to you?

Are you living that way?

Do you know Scripture well enough to be truly loving to those around you?

personal convictions

One man esteems one day as better than another, while another man esteems all days alike [sacred]. Let everyone be fully convinced (satisfied) in his own mind.

ROMANS 14:5, AMP

Sin is not fixed. *What do you mean?* Let's begin by quoting again a section from chapter 5:

> The football game suddenly became just background noise as I stared long and hard at that Henry's label, counting the cost. Five minutes later I stood up, walked to the sink, and poured the beer down the drain. I haven't touched a drop of alcohol since that day.
>
> Is it a sin to drink? No. The Bible is full of references to people drinking wine, even Jesus Himself (see Matthew 11:16-19).

Think back. What did you feel the moment you read that I don't drink alcohol? Did it bug you? Did it make you nervous? Even though I immediately followed my statement by saying I don't think drinking is sin, a personal conviction like this can be troubling, can't it? Actually, I *do* think drinking alcohol is sin—for me, that is.

Hold it! How can it be sin for you if it's not for me?

Easy. God made it a sin for me and not for you. That is why it is called a *personal* conviction. It is something that the Lord has placed off-limits for me personally, and that is scriptural:

But if anyone regards something as unclean, then for him it is unclean. (Romans 14:14)

The Lord has given me other personal convictions as well. One came shortly after I had moved back to Iowa from California. Visiting my family in Cedar Rapids, I bopped into the Plaza 4 Theaters one warm summer evening to catch a movie.

I always loved going to the movies. When I was studying overseas in Maidenhead, England (just west of London), during my junior year at Stanford, I made good use of my BritRail pass. I would hit the movies in London every weekend during the semester, sometimes catching three or four per weekend. When Robert Redford's *The Electric Horseman* came out during my senior year in Palo Alto, I watched it *nine* times over the course of fourteen days. I couldn't get enough of the movies.

Anyway, at the Plaza 4 that evening, I was enjoying the movie immensely until the hero fell asleep and his dream sequence began to play out on the screen. Bloody lambs, bloody crosses, and other blasphemous visuals rolled across the screen. Suddenly I heard a piercing, tortured scream in my spirit in response to those images. Before I knew it, I calmly stood up and walked briskly out of the show, not sure exactly why I was leaving but absolutely certain I should. As I passed through the exit and my feet hit the pavement, I heard the Holy Spirit command, "You will no longer go to theaters."

I didn't even argue. I said, "You got it. I won't." It never occurred to me to question it for a second.

Now, let's stop a moment. This is a weird story, isn't it? And because of the attitudes of Christians toward convictions like this, I risk a lot more in sharing what happened at the Plaza 4 than I do in sharing stories from my racy, pornographic days at Stanford. You don't find too many folks who don't go to the movies, but what I heard that evening was a direct and personal request by my Father.

So I haven't been to the movies since. Yes, I watch videos at home with Brenda and the family, and I have the largest personal collection of television shows and movies of anyone on my block—probably more than a thousand titles, and some now in DVD. I have nothing against movies, and neither does God, as long as they are clean (and as you might imagine, mine are).

But that evening at the Plaza 4, I was asked by my Father not to go to theaters. He made it a *personal* conviction with me. That doesn't mean I feel that it should become a personal conviction for you, and I never will because of this scripture:

So whatever you believe about these things keep between yourself
and God. (Romans 14:22)

To be honest, I would think you to be crazy to follow my convictions if the Holy Spirit hasn't spoken to you about it.

God says that no one else needs to care about my personal convictions but me, and yet many still do. God also says that no one should disrespect my convictions or judge me for them, but I can assure you, I have been judged plenty. *You sound legalistic, Fred.*

That's silly. After all, you read my story…there wasn't anything dead or legalistic about it! It was something between me and the Father, a fresh word spoken through the living Holy Spirit to me, a living testimony of the grace of my living Christ.

But someone else's personal convictions can make you nervous, can't they? You may wonder what's wrong with you. *God spoke to Fred about movies but not to me! Is he more spiritual?*

Not at all. My convictions don't necessarily mean that I'm more spiritual than anyone else. In fact, God may have spoken this word to me because I'm *less* spiritual or because there is some weakness in me. Or He may have spoken to me because a weakness in one of my children might be triggered by witnessing a sensual preview or scene somewhere down the line. Maybe He spoke to me because avoiding theaters would help me grow sexually pure more quickly. Regardless, why should it matter to you? God knows me best, and I not only accept that, I welcome it.

As for you, go ahead and take in a good movie and enjoy a small barrel of popcorn. Let's relax and be happy for one another. There will be no Christian unity until we do. And I guess I should know.

Recently, I gave a large party, and among the guests were two old friends that I've known for over ten years. I invited them graciously into my home, and they sat on my patio and ate my food, all the while soundly mocking the whole concept of avoiding movie theaters quite loudly, though they knew full well my personal convictions on the matter.

I couldn't believe my ears. Their behavior was deeply puzzling to me not only on a *social* level (why would a friend do that?) but also on a *spiritual* level (why would a Christian do that?). In Romans 14, Paul said such behavior is unloving and that it breaks down unity among brothers. And do you know what? Paul was right. It hurt deeply, and I felt trashed and marginalized by these guys.

But while it hurt, and while these questions puzzled me, in the end there is always only one question that matters when it comes to personal convictions: Are you willing to play out your life before an audience of One? We have to live and die by the convictions we have before God, and we have to be willing to risk doing things a little differently from the way everyone else is doing things.

Can God count on you? Can you ignore that larger audience for the sake of that One, your Beloved? You must follow what He's whispered into your heart, whatever the cost. Intimacy with God means oneness with

God, oneness with His character and His ways. Intimacy means hearing and then doing.

Intimacy with others means freeing them to play out their lives before *their* audience of One as well. You must allow them to play out their lives without fear of ridicule and without fear that you'll draw away and ice them socially. Paul says that in the area of personal conviction, you must sacrifice your own tastes to accept your brother and to make room for him, no matter how different. And if you expect total unity, you must defend— yes, even honor—his position before that larger audience of men. Other- wise, you toss a stumbling block of laughter before his faith and his intimacy with God.

Quiz

Are you hounding someone about your personal
   convictions?
Are you mocking another for his personal conviction?
Biblically speaking, do you have a right to do either?

contextual sin

A bruised reed he will not break, and a smoldering wick he will not snuff out, till he leads justice to victory.

MATTHEW 12:20

Because sin isn't fixed, we must not only broaden our definition of sin to match God's, but given what the Bible says about personal convictions, we must also allow our relationships to define sin for us. Things that are not sin within one relationship may very well be sin in the context of another.

We find a great deal to think about this in the clear teaching of the apostle Paul. When discussing in the book of Romans what foods were okay, or "clean," for a Christian to eat, Paul acknowledged that "disputable matters" would be normal in the Christian community. As you read his words, think about how the same is true in a Christian marriage:

Accept him whose faith is weak, without passing judgment on dis-putable matters. One man's faith allows him to eat everything, but another man, whose faith is weak, eats only vegetables. The man who eats everything must not look down on him who does not, and the man who does not eat everything must not condemn the man who does, for God has accepted him. (Romans 14:1-3)

The term *faith* here refers not to saving faith in Christ but to the sense of confidence in one's liberty in Christ. In this case, "strong" Christians, such as Paul, understood that their diet had no spiritual significance. The "weak" simply were not yet clear as to the status of the Old Testament regulations under Christ's New Covenant. The motivations behind both the weak and the strong were the same—both wanted to avoid sin and to serve God fully. The point, Paul said, is that unity among Christians must not be based upon everyone's agreement over disputable questions. Christians won't agree on all matters pertaining to the Christian life, because God didn't address every matter in Scripture. Nor do they need to agree as long as they handle their disputes lovingly.

As an apostle, Paul could have demanded that everyone agree with him. But he chose not to, and asks us to do the same:

Instead, make up your mind not to put any stumbling block or obstacle in your brother's way. As one who is in the Lord Jesus, I am fully convinced that no food is unclean in itself. But...if your brother is distressed because of what you eat, you are no longer acting in love. Do not by your eating destroy your brother for whom Christ died....

Let us therefore make every effort to do what leads to peace and to mutual edification. *Do not destroy the work of God* for the sake of food. All food is clean, but *it is wrong* for a man to eat anything that causes someone else to stumble. *It is better not to eat meat* or drink wine or to do anything else that will cause your brother to fall. (Romans 14:13-15,19-21)

Paul was a brilliant apostle and leader of the Gentile church. Because of his authority, he could have demanded that everyone believe his way regarding food, but he didn't. Instead, Paul submitted to his brother in Christ. In other words, he yielded his right to assert his authority in order to make room for the beliefs of his weaker brother.

Why did he do this? Eating meat was not sin from God's point of view, but it became a sin within the context of Paul's relationship with his brother. To trample that conviction could cause disunity and damage his brother's spirit. It wasn't important to Paul that his brother be like *him*. It was important that his brother become like *Christ*. To be concerned with such trivial matters as food regulations was to miss the essence of Christian living.

How far are you willing to go to illustrate Christ's normal character in this way? Christ was always loving and gentle—he wouldn't break a bruised reed or snuff out a smoldering wick when it came to His relationships with others.

Our presidents are careful in this way. For instance, the president of the United States is the most powerful man on earth. When he invites foreign representatives to the White House, he has the right and the power to choose what he wants to serve at state dinners. Who could argue?

And yet our presidents have been quite sensitive in choosing menus so as not to offend guests who might take issue with eating pork or beef or any number of dishes. President George W. Bush, for instance, is a Texan who loves steak, and he sees nothing wrong with enjoying a thick T-bone. But while he is freed by his conscience to eat this kind of meat, he is aware that others are repulsed and violently opposed to eating a juicy steak.

So he doesn't serve up New York strips to such guests. He knows that his most important mission is to protect the harmony between the United States and the nations of visiting dignitaries.

A leader who gives up his right to choose? Why would he sacrifice like this? He doesn't have to. After all, with the position come the perks, right? President Bush could demand that everyone eat like he eats, quelling the controversy by edict. He has the right to have things his way.

Yet to him, giving up his right to choose the meat on the menu is an easy call when his real goal is pursuing the higher call of world unity. He figures a good leader should be willing to adjust his behavior for the sake of his friends. He understands that pressing his rights at the expense of friendship and oneness is wrong.

Why is it wrong? Take a look. If he demands his way, what does he gain? He gets to eat his meat freely, but visiting dignitaries would be violating their consciences with every bite. He may have his way, but he doesn't have their hearts. Instead, he's trampling them.

For the president this leadership principle seems wise and makes perfect sense to any of us. Unity is important, but in our marriages and in our relationships within the church, this same thinking can seem way outside the box!

Contrast the attitudes of Paul and our president to that of this husband who refused to give up his "right" to a female friend. His wife gave us a copy of the letter she wrote to him:

I could never get you to understand how much your friendship with Janie was hurting our relationship. In her you found a confidante, someone who agreed with you. You chose sharing with her over sharing with me. You didn't want to come home and instead spent extra hours at work. You chose to have lunch with her to discuss personal issues together. You began to say things to me at home like, "Janie understands… Janie agrees… Janie thinks…" You even visited her one evening while her husband was out of town. You called to talk to her when you were in our home, even though you knew it hurt me.

When I called to talk to you at work, she would take the phone and tell me how I should be raising my son and how I should be listening to you. She made it clear how much she likes you and how difficult I'm being as a wife to you. You would never listen to me. Emotionally, I broke down. When I started doing crazy things and losing so much weight, I went to the doctor and cried my guts out in his office. I just could not deal with the pain. I was on the verge of a nervous breakdown. Only then did you begin to realize my state of mind and finally break off your friendship with her, but you have never let me forget that I made you lose your buddy.

Having a female friend is not sin, per se, but within the context of *this* relationship, it was way out of bounds, and this husband's actions bruised someone who didn't deserve to be trampled the way she was.

Quiz

Could it be said of you that "a bruised reed he will not break, and a smoldering wick he will not snuff out"?
Are you allowing the Spirit to cultivate the fruit of gentleness and kindness in you?

painting pictures

*I pray also for those who will believe in me through their mes-
sage, that all of them may be one, Father.... May they be brought
to complete unity to let the world know that you sent me and
have loved them even as you have loved me.*

JOHN 17:20-21,23

Many want to call fewer things sin, as this reader wrote us:

> You know, Fred, sometimes your talk about leading "holy and blame-
> less lives," while absolutely commanded, sounds rather dull. Maybe
> it's my background, I don't know. I've grown up in church, and when
> I hear those terms, it conjures up certain feelings I can't describe.
> That's because I feel that certain "restrictions" on behavior are dis-
> tasteful to me.

Some view sin as a bossy mother with crossed arms and arched eyebrow
scolding, "You'd better not do that anymore, or your Father will have your
hide!"

But we don't think God intended this at all, and if you've won your victory over sexual sin, you are certain of this as well. Sure, sin has power, and

it has darkness behind it to destroy us. God never forgets this, and we shouldn't either.

That being said, God doesn't want us calling more things sin because He's some kind of control freak out to rope in our lives. On the contrary, He wants to free us to live life abundantly. Giving us a broader, more accurate view of sin does just that.

Think about it. Why did He give us His Law in the first place? Not to rule us, but to teach us:

Through the law we become conscious of sin. (Romans 3:20)

How can we know what is right or wrong without the Law? We can't. But even more to the point, how else can we know what's normal so we can walk normally in the midst of our relationships without trampling those around us?

Both Jesus (see Matthew 22:36-39) and Paul reveal that the Law was never about guilt and shame in the first place. It was always entirely about relationships:

You, my brothers, were called to be free. But do not use your freedom to indulge the sinful nature; rather, serve one another in love. The entire law is summed up in a single command: "Love your neighbor as yourself." If you keep on biting and devouring each other, watch out or you will be destroyed by each other. (Galatians 5:13-15)

God doesn't want you to feel guilty about your behavior as much as He wants you to urgently want to change. This is the age of grace. Christ has won. Calling sin, sin is not about heaven and hell anymore.

Rather, it's about relationships. It's about the pictures you're painting of

Him with your life, and the picture of Christ's love that you're showing the world as you interact with your friends and family. A broader, more accurate view of sin isn't meant to be your shock collar or even your baby-sitter. In God's hands the Law is meant to be your kind mentor, teaching you what is normal and how to love your neighbor. The Law teaches you to paint lovely pictures of Christ in your relationships so all men will know that you are His disciple and that all men might be drawn to Him.

If you're wondering what sin has to do with loving those around you, the apostle John has your answer:

> This is how we know that we love the children of God: by…carrying out his commands. (1 John 5:2)

When we obey God's commands, we love those around us. To us, Scripture couldn't be clearer. God's purposes on earth couldn't be clearer either. These pictures and these relationships are everything to our Father. He wants us to obey for His sake, that He might draw His children home when they see Him in us. He wants us to obey for our own sake so that we don't warp ourselves or *our* children. That way they can see Him in us.

After all, what was that new command He gave us? That we love one another so that all men would know we are His disciples (see John 13:34-35). And what was His final prayer before heading out to Gethsemane? That God would make us one so that the whole world might believe (see John 17:20-21).

He wants you to be a fine artist, normal and Christlike in all your ways. When you aren't, the pictures drawn by your relationships are spoiled by sin, spawning pain, unrest, and confusion in those around you. This draws no one to Christ. Gaze upon a picture spoiled by a husband's sin:

> My husband is a chief of a military base, and many are watching him because he is a Christian. Sadly, I recently discovered porn on his

computer and confronted him about it. He admitted to me that he struggles with porn, and he asked me to pray for him.

At first he seemed repentant, but he wasn't really sorry for what he did. I've asked him to get off the Internet, and he has at least done that. I've asked him to go to church regularly, but he's only gone once. I've asked him to read *Every Man's Battle,* but he has not done that. I've asked him to find another man to share *everything* with. He hasn't talked to anyone. I see no change in him at all. He goes from wanting to act like nothing is wrong to making me think *I'm* the one with the problem and wanting me to feel sorry for him! The reality is that he wants to do things his way, not God's way.

What a picture! Sure, this man may love his wife *emotionally.* But he isn't obeying God's commands, and so he isn't loving his wife *in practice.* Naturally, she doesn't *feel* loved and feels no unity with him. Living a holy and blameless life is not dull, distasteful, and restricting. It is the only path to real love, real peace, and real life.

Contrast that soiled picture with this one:

I never knew I was getting a sexual high from looking at other women—even with my wife standing right there. I sensed that my checking out other women bothered her, but I dismissed those feelings. I am a touchy-feely type person who likes to give hugs to females, and I love to flirt with waitresses and even my wife's friends.

A while back, I took my wife on a date. I'd been reading your book over and over for the previous two months, so I had dabbled a bit in going cold turkey with my eyes, but I've got to tell you that the devil plays hardball. I felt like a failure every time I'd catch myself.

Anyway, I'd just read again the section about whether or not to tell your wife. I wanted to tell her how I was struggling to control how I looked at women and how I didn't want to fail at this. I thought she could help me, but I was afraid to tell her because I thought I might fail.

But on our date, my wife knew something was up, so she asked me if anything was bothering me. I told her about what I'd been reading in *Every Man's Battle,* and then I somehow scrounged up the courage to ask her for help. I grabbed the book off the backseat and let her read about how guys are scared they could fail and how ashamed they are to tell their wives about their struggles.

My wife took it really well. In fact, she was excited. She told me how she'd been praying for a number of weeks that God would open my heart about what I do with my eyes, and she explained how badly it hurts her. I couldn't believe it!

I then let my wife read what happens when purity comes and my full desire is transferred to her. By then we were at the restaurant, and when we reached our table, we began discussing things we have never talked about before in fourteen years of marriage.

We even talked—a very little—about how sometimes I think about my ex-wife (we were married for a short period twenty years ago), wondering what she looks like and wondering if I'd still be married to her if I knew then what I know now. We talked about this for two hours in a calm manner, and then we talked about our sexual needs in ways we never have before.

My wife has now read much of the rest of the book and is really helping me out. She has even initiated sex for me regularly to help me stay pure.

Isn't this a transforming picture? He's obeying God's commands, and in so doing, he is loving his wife. She feels love and unity, and she is loving him in return by obeying God's commands and fighting the good fight with him.

Both these men began in the same sin, but one wanted urgently to change and to walk normally like Jesus.

And that's a great picture.

Quiz

What pictures are you painting with your marriage? Stone walls and stalemates?

What has your wife been saying about your "artistry"? Is she aching, or is she "ah-ing" at its beauty?

How about your neighbors?

sophistication versus sanctification

Sanctification is the process by which a man becomes normal in the context of the kingdom of God. The more sanctified you are, the more the fruit of the Spirit will grow freely, and the more normal you will seem to other Christians:

> But the fruit of the Spirit is love, joy, peace, patience, kindness, goodness, faithfulness, gentleness and self-control. (Galatians 5:22-23)

Sophistication, on the other hand, is the process by which a man becomes normal in the context of the world. The more sophisticated you are, the more normal you'll look to the pagans. You'll fit right into their world.

The fruits of sophistication include lust, faithlessness, selfishness, self-absorption, and the love of money. The fruit of sophistication rots the fruit of the Spirit.

As you live in this victory over sexual sin and move deeper into your walk with Christ, selflessness should be growing in the marriage bed. In fact, the Golden Rule should be evident in a uniquely literal sense…you love her as you would like to be loved yourself.

As real, true intimacy grows to replace the false intimacy of sexual sin, you should find that you care more and more about her physical pleasure. If you haven't found that yet, you need to actively move in that direction. Ask her how you are doing.

You should also be connecting more deeply with her *spiritually* and *emotionally* in the marriage bed by now. Some of this will happen naturally because your sexual sin has created, after all, an adulterous wall between your spirits in the spirit realm, a wall that has now crumbled. Your spirits are meeting consistently and fully in the marriage bed for the first time, and this change will automatically be reflected in your relationship together.

Some of it won't happen naturally, however, and will require transformation through conscious meditation upon Scripture and the washing of the Word as your "sophisticated" roots are replaced by Christ's normal ways in your approach to your wife and your sexual intimacy.

sophistication I

There is a way that seems right to a man, but in the end it leads to death.

PROVERBS 14:12

By the time he was seventy-two years old, my dad was dying from congestive heart problems and kidney disease. The medication for one would exacerbate the other, so although he underwent surgery to buy some time, it didn't work. I knew he was failing. Even with his oxygen tank he couldn't walk fifteen feet without stopping to catch his breath. It was hard to see this Superman, this former national wrestling champion and bulldog of a businessman fade away in such a demeaning, sapping fashion.

I could feel that he was getting close to the end, so during a visit just a few weeks before his death, I knew this might be the last time I'd see him alive. I had a question buried deep in my heart, buried decades earlier in the dusty rubble and debris of my parents' divorce, a question born of torturous confusion and measureless pain.

Before I could ask him that question, my thoughts turned back to that day when the sun dimmed and never shone as brightly again—the day I learned that Mom was divorcing Dad, who'd been playing around with another woman for quite some time. I recalled how painful that was to me, an eleven-year-old boy who wanted only love from his mother and father—not bitter arguments and tumultuous rancor. I watched as Mom, feeling so much shame and pain, cried for hours because my father turned his back on her to fall into the arms of another woman.

As I sat in Dad's living room that day and made small talk, I remembered the only time that he had talked to me about the divorce. We had been standing by some elevators at the Cheyenne Mountain Resort in Colorado Springs a few years earlier. He was waiting for my stepmother while I waited for Brenda. We happened to be attending a national convention for the company we both worked for, but this one convention promised to be something special: Dad was retiring after thirty-eight years with the company (I had been with the same company for ten years). I don't know if it was because of the emotions that a man feels as he faces retirement and looks back over the years, but Dad pulled me aside with tears in his eyes—and my father wasn't one to get weepy. He said, "Freddie, there has been something I've been wanting to tell you for a while, and now, since I'm retiring, I've just got to tell you."

"Sure, Dad. What's up?"

"You know our divorce?"

What sort of question was that? That would be like asking me if I ever heard of September 11. Of course, I knew about his divorce. I nodded for him to continue.

"I just want you to know that that divorce was the stupidest mistake I ever made in my life. Your mom was a good woman, and I threw her away. And do you know what? I never recovered from that mistake, no matter how hard I tried. I never recovered financially, no matter how hard I worked. I never had another relationship any better than the one I had with your mom, though I've known many women. And worst of all, I've never been able to really rebuild my relationships with you kids like I wanted to because of the pain of that divorce."

I was stunned. Dad had never talked this openly about his mistakes before. I cried and we hugged, and I forgave him and told him I was sorry he'd never recovered.

That moment meant so much to me, but I still didn't know *why* he had forsaken his wedding vows, a question that had burned in my heart since elementary school. Ever since that moment ten years earlier, I'd hoped for a chance to open that topic once more. On this occasion, as I greeted my dying father in his home, I took a seat in the living room while he rested on a couch.

When I was younger I was too scared of his thunderous moods to ask him why he divorced my mom. When I reached my twenties, I'd chicken out, always saying, "Maybe next time." Then came the long years of stalemate, when I never saw him and couldn't ask. On this day, though, I knew it was time. He was too weak to thunder, and it was too late to chicken out. Sitting on his end of the couch, rasping and gasping, he knew the curtain was about to fall. So I asked him, choking just a bit in fear and respect.

"Why, Dad? Why did you divorce her? You were married to a good woman; you said so yourself in Colorado Springs. You told me that it wrecked your relationship with your kids and that you never recovered from it. Is there something you haven't told me? Did Mom have an affair first, so you retaliated?"

Dad shook his head no.

"Was she secretly a witch to live with, or were there problems in bed? What was going through your head?"

My father looked off in the distance as he contemplated what he should say. "I don't know, Freddie," he began. "It just seemed like the thing to do back then. This happened during the early days of the Playboy generation. Having a mistress was just the thing men did to prove they were with it, with the times. Sophisticated. I never really thought it through. That's really all it was."

I was dumbfounded. *It was just the thing men did? You took a mistress and never really thought it through? That was the reason for all this?*

We were silent for a long moment. Mercifully, he managed to change the subject, and I was only too grateful. Before long, we finished up, and I headed out for the long ride home to Des Moines.

As the miles melted behind me, I thought about the other occasions when my father had proposed an idea that he probably read first in "Playboy Forum." When I was fourteen (remember, my parents were divorced at this time), Dad called Mom early one week and gave her the following order: "Have Freddie ready for me to pick up Friday night at seven o'clock. I've got a clean prostitute arranged for the evening. It's time for him to learn about love."

Mom and I, after determining that he was really serious, were repulsed by the bizarre idea. But that's what Dad thought sexually sophisticated fathers did for their newly adolescent sons. And since he was cool when it came to sexual matters, his son needed to become cool as well.

Other memories cruised in as well, including crushing memories from the painful, churning wake of the divorce. I thought back to the day Mom was hospitalized by the financial pressure after the divorce…how my dad had held up child support for eight months to punish her or, in his words, "to break her." I remember having to move from our comfortable house in an upscale development to a cramped little house on Cedar Rapid's west side…how we kids tried to be brave, but near the end of our first tour of our homely, dumpy house, all four of us just sat down in a circle and cried. I remembered what I called the Suicidal Years, when my sisters just couldn't recover and never felt loved… I remembered the terror of driving the thirty miles from Cedar Rapids to Iowa City at 120 miles per hour at the age of seventeen, desperately hoping to get to my sister's apartment before she killed herself. She'd hung up the phone after saying it was over, and I didn't know what I'd find. Gratefully, she answered the door sleepily, having faded off under the waves of emotional exhaustion before doing anything. *All these things! And he never really thought about it?*

How shameful of my dad for what he did to my mother and my family. Sure, he paid his price, and what's done is done. I forgave him, but his actions were still shameful and cruel. Remember what he said: "It was just the thing we all did back then."

Who was "we"? Well, it was the popular culture—guys reading *Playboy* and drinking highballs and ignoring their wives and children while they were out clubbing. All because it was cool and sophisticated.

What a crock that turned out to be. Which brings us to a very important question for all of us men: What are you doing just because everyone else is doing it—or says it's okay?

If I had to hazard a guess, I would say that we're looking at seductive female bodies in our mainstream media—the television, the Internet, and magazines. And if that stuff is pumping into the recesses of your mind, then you could be following in my father's footsteps, polluting your home and your marriage bed.

Sophistication has warped your view of normal, and if you are like my dad, you may not even know it. It is every man's challenge to root out sophistication and to return to innocence, to allow God's truth to transform, reshape, and sanctify our minds that we might stand and think normally before God. That we might act normally, sexually and otherwise, with our wives. That we might think normally before our families and all men.

But how? His Word is speaking, and the Spirit is calling. Listen carefully and be quick to answer. Are you too sophisticated? Do you have baggage? Wherever the Spirit points, choose change.

And above all, intercede for yourself. Do you know what my deepest cry to God has become, the cry that burns, the one that draws sobs from my heart and tears from my eyes every time? *Oh, God, please don't leave me like this. I want more of You. Please don't leave me like this!*

Find the cry of *your* heart, the one that burns. Then grab God around the waist in prayer and refuse to let go of Him until you have it.

Quiz

Is your view of divorce sophisticated or is it normal?
Does your heart burn for a return to innocence?

sophistication II

*Dear friends, this is now my second letter to you. I have written
both of them as reminders to stimulate you to wholesome thinking.*

2 PETER 3:1

While floods of bad memories rolled over me as I drove home to Des Moines after talking to my dad about the divorce that day, the only emotion that came to me was wry bemusement. Every five or ten miles after another wave of memories, I'd just chuckle, shaking my head with half-curled, half-pursed lips, muttering to myself, "Typical. Just typical. Isn't that typical of life, all this painful ado out of nothing, out of a nondecision. He didn't even think it through!"

Maybe I should have felt anger, but all I could do was laugh at life's cruel joke on me. "Why should I be surprised?" I muttered. At the age of thirty, or maybe thirty-five, I'd have blown up. But by now I'd taken enough solid pastings from life that all I could do was grin wryly and mutter, "Okay, you got me again, Life. Deal 'em up again. I'll get you next time."

My dad blundered into the dumbest decision of his life, by his own admission, all because he thought having a mistress was cool. He did so without stopping to question his actions or his definition of *sophisticated.* He got cool, but he also got so blind that he couldn't see that his actions were so inherently silly that even his eleven-year-old son could see how stupid they were at the time. Later that same innocent, eleven-year-old son—me—would move into his own sexually sophisticated world without uttering a question himself. Talk about dumb and dumber.

We all begin sexually innocent, but after getting dunked into the River of Puberty, most of us bob and float downstream, carried along and gaining more and more understanding—and sexual sophistication—along the way. Asking few questions, we just keep floating merrily along, picking up whatever surface debris and scum that happen to stick.

One of the reasons we never make it to full purity is that we bring our warped, sophisticated views into our marriage bed. They never really die, and they continue splashing up and over the edges of our lives, keeping us vulnerable to sin and temptation.

What about you? Have you ever wondered in what ways your sophistication has blinded you? Maybe you're sure you could never become involved in an affair. Fair enough. But are you hurting your wife with your sophisticated ways, just the same? It's worth posing the question, something that my father should have done. That's something all of us should do when it comes to sophistication.

We need to think wholesomely about our life behind closed doors. So let me ask you a few questions:

- What do you know about male and female sexual response?
- Would you say that you're fairly sophisticated in your views?
- If so, how did you become so sophisticated?

You probably didn't become enlightened on your own. Someone or *something* filled in the blanks for you along the way. These days that someone is usually a premarital sex partner and that *something* is usually pornography in its various forms.

Premarital sex is all me-me by definition, because it's all about gaining sexual pleasure without any long-term commitment. If things aren't working out how you expected in bed, or if you get bored with the relationship, then it's *hasta la vista,* baby.

With or without a steady girlfriend, there are always honeys available on the Internet, soft- and hard-core magazines, or PG-13–rated (and beyond) movies. Looking, staring, and wondering lead to lusting, which leads to fantasy, which leads to masturbation. You literally take your sexual pleasure into your own hands and get used to the idea that your sexuality was created for you. It wasn't.

Then you get married. That would be okay, except you bring into your marriage all of your sophisticated views and habits of sexuality. That could include the time you heard a guest on *Oprah* declare that a hot movie (like *Eyes Wide Shut* a few years back with Tom Cruise and Nicole Kidman) can spice up a marriage and even "liberate" it. You nod your head because you've heard stuff like this said before. Your attitude may parallel that of David, a Christian, who expressed this experience after watching the movie *The Thomas Crown Affair:*

> Well, I have a right to watch whatever I want. I'm an American, and I have the liberty to do what I want. This movie was so, so sensual that my wife and I had the hottest sex we had in quite a while. That was good enough for me.

Fine. But that doesn't make it right, nor does it make it the *best.* Sure, this guy increased his *physical* satisfaction for one evening. Big deal! Any college student could have predicted that would happen. That's Human Sexuality 101—the longer the buildup of sexual tension during foreplay, the more intense the orgasm. What better way to stretch out that foreplay than to gather together in the darkness with popcorn and watch a sophisticated, tension-building, visual lovemaking scene? Watching others have sex in a classy movie early in the evening can heat up passions later on, especially when you place the starlet's face over your wife's as you make love to her. A little variety never hurt, right?

Wrong, and it's wrong for a deep reason. You simply aren't one in heart with your wife when you do this. When the evening's over, you've had some fun in bed with her, but your eyes and your heart were never centered on her. How can your souls meet when you are cheating in your mind? I found I couldn't meet Brenda's soul in bed under these circumstances. Odds are, neither can you. Could that possibly fit God's picture?

Well, she doesn't mind. She watches these movies with me!

Whether she minds is not the question. She may not even be aware that you can get an erection from watching a sex scene.

What matters is that sex is not just physical, although many "sophisticated" adults go their whole lives without experiencing sex beyond the physical level. The emotions and the soul can be intensely involved in the marriage bed and impact the sexual experience far beyond foreplay's limits. But in a typical paradox, like many found in God's kingdom, I've found that meeting my wife's soul in the pure integrity of my heart has increased our physical pleasure together.

But too many take shelter in our so-called sophistication and bring it to bed with us. And we approach sex with our wives with the same idea we approached sex with ourselves and with our fantasies: *As long as it's good for me, it is good.* We assume she's happy if we're happy, yet how can we know? Our only training came from masturbation, movies, and a few illicit trysts along the way. We assume that the physical blast is all there is. We wouldn't know or understand God's plan for sex if it bit us.

Quiz

Does your wife think you know very much about female sexual response? This is too important to leave to guesswork. Why don't you ask her?

trampling her bed

Let your gentleness be evident to all. The Lord is near.

PHILIPPIANS 4:5

Readers of *Every Man's Battle* have bombed us with e-mails asking a variation of this question: "How can I get my wife to desire sex with me?"

That's a great question. Let's begin by looking at sexual desire from a woman's point of view. Connie wrote this to us:

> My husband recently read *Every Man's Marriage*, and since he isn't usually very communicative about his views on marriage, I chose to read the book, too, in hopes of gaining some new insight. Not being a man, I can't speak to every aspect of this book, but as a Christian, I want to speak to you about one particular portion of the book that I found very disturbing.
>
> I was greatly bothered by your reference to 1 Corinthians 7:2-5, which says, "The husband should fulfill his marital duty to his wife, and likewise the wife to her husband." You apparently take this to mean that a woman is obligated to satisfy her husband's sexual desires whether she wants to or not. Should this obligation to provide sexual fulfillment override my desire to avoid pain? Let me describe my situation.

I have now been married for almost a year to the only guy I ever dated, and I've never had sexual contact with anyone else. I love him very much; he is my brother in Christ and my best friend. But my romantic feelings for him have pretty much flat-lined because he ignores me romantically and, in my opinion, abuses me sexually.

I probably ought to back up a little and explain. When we first began dating, and up until our engagement, Rich treated me with great consideration. We had long conversations, and the thing I liked most was that we laughed together. As we dated longer and longer, there were many expressions of affection, both verbally and through hugs and kisses. We prayed together, too, although not nearly as often as I would have liked.

Then something strange happened after I accepted Rich's proposal. He began to treat me as though I were silly, and he began to disregard my opinions on important decisions that affected our future together. For example, I wanted a small wedding that would not severely strain my parents' disability income, but when Rich's parents insisted on having a large guest list, he would not support me by asking for a streamlined version from them. And so on down the line.

I don't think that female submission means that a woman should be treated as stupid, especially when she has been blessed with plenty of intelligence. My God-given intelligence could help him, I guarantee it! Anyway, once he had that ring on my finger, it was as if he no longer had to woo me to get what he wanted, so why bother? He started doing whatever he wanted, whether I liked it or not. And now, since our wedding, that same attitude has pretty well defined our sexual relationship.

I have read that a strong sexual bond can strengthen a man's attachment to his wife, and that is why I have submitted to Rich's sexual desire on every occasion but one. The fact that I have several medical conditions undoubtedly contributes to my own lack of physical desire, but I know that I am capable of sexual feelings because I have struggled with sexual temptation in relation to another man (who I am currently avoiding because of this).

In any case, I am not terribly disturbed that Rich fails to arouse my physical desire. Given my busy life, I certainly have more on my mind than achieving orgasms. What upsets me is that he really doesn't do much of anything to help make having sex with him tolerable.

As I mentioned before, the most fulfilling aspects of our relationship have pretty well disappeared. Calling out, "Hey, you're a babe" when I pass through the room as he endlessly channel-surfs hardly measures up to actually taking the time to pray with me after a hard day at work. Yet he seems to expect me to be turned on every time we touch.

Lately, I think he has been experimenting with talking in bed because he read somewhere that women find that to be sexy, but that hasn't impressed me at all. Nor has growling "Yeah, baby" while applying bruising pressure to my breast or other body parts.

I am fine with not having an orgasm. But I'm not sure how much longer I can or should take the kind of treatment I am getting from my "godly" husband (publicly, anyway). I don't feel loved or cherished in our marriage bed; instead, I feel that I have been trapped and assaulted. I am tired of submitting to sex almost daily and, very often, more than once a day, even when I am menstruating. I desperately want to be a good and godly wife, but I just don't see how 1 Corinthians 7:2-5 obligates me to do all that I've been doing. In fact, I feel more distant from my husband every time he tramples over me in this way.

I can accept that Rich may never be a good lover, no matter how many supposedly helpful books he reads. Intercourse may never last longer than fifteen to twenty seconds for us, and Rich may always find it too exciting to resist digging his fingers into my flesh…I can live with that. But I have great difficulty accepting that I will be married to a man who tramples my essence almost nightly for as long as his virility holds out.

I am seriously thinking of giving up this battle. Rich has, in some measure, stripped my heart to a wasteland. I honestly do not feel obligated by Scripture to continue pleasuring him in this way. After all, why can't Rich live without sex if I'm forced to live without romance?

Most of us men care more about our sex life than we do about following God's Word regarding how we should treat our wives in the bedroom. Yet when God writes, "Her body is not her own," we read, "She's my sex toy. I'll serve her everywhere else, but here she'll serve me!"

But she isn't your sex toy. To think that way is to twist God's Word. And it is the main reason why sexual oneness has died in so many Christian marriages. Demeaned wives draw back sexually because God never intended for them to carry the burden of sexual fulfillment that their husbands have laid on them.

God never talks about sex in the context of one person, and He did not give us our sexuality for ourselves. He gave us our sexuality for our partner:

The husband should fulfill his marital duty to his wife, and likewise the wife to her husband. The wife's body does not belong to her alone but also to her husband. In the same way, the husband's body does not belong to him alone but also to his wife. (1 Corinthians 7:3-4)

Sex is not about you. Your sexuality exists in the relationship for her pleasure, and her sexuality exists in the relationship for yours. While sexual self-focus is normal everywhere else, it is abnormal in the Christian marriage bed.

I once asked my marriage class a series of questions:

- How is your relationship with your spouse different, now that it includes sex, compared to before marriage, when it did not?
- What has it done for your relationship?
- Are there things that sex can do that nothing else can do for your relationship?

Here are some answers I received from the ladies:

- *Vanna:* "Sex helps break down pride and independence in relation to my husband."
- *Samantha:* "Sex provides a special oneness and a refuge of tranquility."
- *Christie:* "Sex teaches you how to rely and depend upon your spouse."
- *Brynna:* "Sex provides one special thing that only you two share together—no one else knows the details."
- *Stacey:* "Sex provides a special place where harmony is never more perfect, and a relaxed atmosphere in which to talk freely and openly."

Now look back through that list and replace the word *sex* with the word *worship* and replace the words *spouse* and *husband* with the word *Lord.* Marriage is a picture of Christ's relationship to the church, and sex is to have the same pure, exciting intimacy as worship does. In worship that intimacy blossoms from a focus on Christ. In sex that intimacy comes from a pure focus upon your wife's soul.

If sex is to bring oneness and intimacy, what should never be found in the marriage bed?

- frustration
- fantasy
- feeling rushed
- feeling pressure to do something uncomfortable

If your sexuality has been given to you primarily for your partner's sake (and not for your own), what commitment *should* be there? For openers, your wife's climax should be as important as your own. Your knowledge of what makes her feel good should be as deep as your knowledge of what makes you feel good.

Have you studied her responses? Are you going slow enough? If she can't respond sexually in the early morning, are you waiting until nightfall?

Her sexuality is tied to her emotions. Have you found her emotional heart of passion? Rachel told me, "I know this sounds strange, but when I see Bill out struggling and toiling with the rototiller in the garden, it really heats me up sexually. I know he hates gardening. I know he's working hard out there so I don't have to do it and solely because he loves me. He cares about our relationship, and that really turns me on."

Compatibility is not necessary for oneness—sacrifice is. Each of us must sacrificially treat our wife's need for romantic fulfillment exactly as we expect her to sacrificially treat our need for sexual fulfillment (see Ephesians 5:33). It's a two-way street, but if you will walk carefully with her on the romantic side, you might be surprised how she'll race with you in your lane.

Quiz

Are you trampling your wife in bed?
Are you man enough to ask your wife this question?

desires and appetites

For a time is coming when people will no longer listen to right teaching. They will follow their own desires and will look for teachers who will tell them whatever they want to hear.

2 TIMOTHY 4:3, NLT

Who have you been listening to, God or the world? If you have been listening to the world, you're hearing that there really is nothing you can do about your drives or appetites. They are just part of you, and these feelings are real. If these desires ask to be satisfied, you must yield to these yearnings and just go for it—every time.

The world was coming in loud and clear when I (Steve) was growing up, especially that part about my tremendous sex drive being a natural, good thing. I wanted some kind of sexual experience every day of my life. During one stretch as an adolescent, it was a rare day when that didn't happen.

I was proud of my sex drive. The way I saw it, I was a real man who wasn't easily satisfied. So my desire for women just grew and grew. Yet sadly, there was something else developing just as rapidly right alongside my sex drive.

During much of my life, I lived in the lonely world of disconnection, and my abilities to separate and alienate myself from others became an art form. I lacked the ability to bond with anyone because I wasn't willing to share who I really was with anyone. Every day I was busier and busier with building the facade of who I thought I was supposed to be or, more precisely, who I thought I was supposed to look like. As a superficially connected person, I sought out superficial relationships with people who were just as disconnected to others as they were with me. Unfortunately, the loneliness became so intense that I sometimes wondered if life was really worth living.

I became a loveless, disconnected man who used women and sex to feel some sort of connection. As long as I was involved with someone sexually, at least I felt involved with someone at some level. But having sex never satisfied my need for real connection, and I often left the encounter feeling empty and afraid.

Then a miracle happened: Someone fell in love with me, and I fell in love with her. When that genuine love experience occurred, I felt my soul beginning to heal. True love does that. Love brought out the best in me and freed me to share my insecurities. Love beat down the path to my heart, and I was willing to be vulnerable and to connect with another person, which was amazing. Life became rich and deep. My relationship was so fulfilling that there was no desire to rush into sex because a fulfilled soul doesn't need instant gratification. True love really can wait, because there's no rush to return to the empty pit of superficial gratification.

Eventually our love was experienced in a physical way, but I was still amazed at how easily I could control my sex drive. It became manageable rather than something that managed me. I was no less male, just a male in control of himself. When that relationship ended, and I began to date others, I did not try to have sex. When that happened, I would walk away at the end of the evening feeling like a million dollars. I gave rather than took and connected rather than controlled. I knew her better from the inside rather than just touching the surface of who she was. Those experiences were nothing short of divine, as God said it would be in 2 Peter 1:4: "By that same mighty power, he has given us all of his rich and wonderful promises. He has promised that you will escape the decadence all around you caused by evil desires and that you will share in his divine nature" (NLT).

If you are *not* escaping the decadence all around you—listening to the world tell you what you want to hear—then you aren't living in His mighty power sharing in His divine nature. I want that for you. I want you to have the supernatural experience of being completely known by another person and being unconditionally loved by her. For that to happen, you will have to do a very scary thing. You will have to step out of yourself and get interested in her life. You will have to put away everything you do to gratify your sexual desires and allow them to return to their normal place. This may seem impossible to you. If that's true, then you haven't been willing to surrender your life to God's truth. That is when the connection can be made and your life can be lived to the fullest.

Quiz

Do you carry painful baggage into all your relationships that affects each one with the same destructive pattern?

How far are you willing to go to dump your baggage and walk normally?

sex with the tent

So I tell you this, and insist on it in the Lord, that you must no longer live as the Gentiles do, in the futility of their thinking.

EPHESIANS 4:17

Brenda and I recently visited our friends Greg and Heather, and as the kids chased Mario and Luigi through the hills and dales of Nintendo, we parents sat together talking and laughing into the night. Brenda looked great to me, and four or five times I looked at her and thought, *I can't wait to get her into my arms later.*

Look, I'm a guy. I'll be visual until the day I die. Whenever I step out of the master bath in the morning and catch her still in her lingerie, I'll murmur breathlessly, "Is NASCAR running this early, or is that the racing of my heart?"

But for too many of us, our sexuality is dominated by our eyes, even after we get them bouncing and under control. While we would never say it to our wives, our attitude is clear: *Okay, I've gotten my eyes under control, and you are looking better than ever before! I've done my part. I've gotten rid of my porn stash and stopped looking at the hotties in the string bikinis. But you have to do your part, babe. Become one of them! Always thin. Always available. Always smiling with that come-on look, ready for action. Become what I've given up for you!*

At best, we want a seductive tigress on the prowl, someone whose wardrobe is provided courtesy of Victoria's Secret. At worst, we want our wife to just lie back and be our own warm, interactive, inflatable doll. We want a sexual well that we can draw from at will.

Our problem? There's been no underlying transformation of our corrupted, "sophisticated" sexuality. Our sexuality is still not about our wives. It is still not about a cherishing inner connection. No, it is still about us and our eyes. It is still about outer beauty and our pleasure.

There is nothing wrong with outer beauty, and it will always have its allure. But outer beauty should not dominate our sexuality, and neither should our eyes, although they often do, as this e-mail attests:

> My husband tells me that he has never found me beautiful enough for him and that it makes him want to leave me and wish he had never married me. In the same breath, he says there is nothing he dislikes about me. In fact, he says I am very attractive, but just not enough. He has constantly looked at other women all our married life.

While most husbands are not as bad as this guy, far too many are simply lighter shades of this same dark pattern. For instance, I was recently at a party when one of the wives sat down with a lovely piece of chocolate cake. Her husband, clearly annoyed, asked sarcastically, "Are you eating *again?*" Later this woman confessed to some friends that her husband is absolutely fanatical about her weight and how it affects his sexual desire for her, and yet she is off the charts in sweetness, joy, and fun. There's so much to desire there.

Is this the best we can do? We were created to walk in the image of Christ, for heaven's sakes! Is this all the better we can stumble along? This is simply not godly…it's putrid. Our visual side may be a natural part of our sexuality, but it is not our *only* side and certainly not how God created us to walk. An exclusive focus on outer beauty bears little resemblance to a God who always looks first at the inside—at a man's heart. This outer focus is very much beneath us as men of God.

But our sophistication and our past warp our tastes and our view of normal. Brandon sent me this letter:

> When Michele and I were married, she was a slender yet full-bodied woman who knocked my socks off! After two years of marriage, however, she started to gain weight. I said some things that hurt her deeply, which just added fuel to the fire. When she gained even more weight, that sent me into depression.
>
> You see, ever since I was a little boy I pictured my future wife as a slender knockout who I would be not only in love with forever, but be in lust with forever. Once she started packing more pounds, I began looking at other women in magazines, movies, and the Internet.
>
> Will the principles in *Every Man's Battle* help me with this particular problem? What if my wife becomes obese? She's not there yet, but what if she gains even *more* weight? Would I still find her attractive by applying these principles?

Yes, you would. Brenda is sixty pounds heavier (don't worry—she gave me permission to say that) than she was on our wedding day, yet she is absolutely, stunningly sensual to me. (In the interest of fairness, I'm no longer at my old football-playing weight either.) As we said in *Every Man's Battle*, if you eliminate the Hollywood images from your viewfinder, your wife becomes your yardstick of beauty because she is all you're looking at. When she's the only thing you allow your eyes to see, and she's the only babe in the cupboard, she'll knock your socks off, believe me.

My wife is amazed at how I yearn for her. She certainly knows she doesn't look the same as she used to, but she's not complaining. And my natural desire does wonders for her self-esteem.

We are commanded to always be ravished by the wife of our youth. How is that possible if we keep looking at buxom young babes all the time? We can't, so we must follow Job's advice and stop looking lustfully at them (see Job 31:1).

As we do, something interesting happens. I've found that as I've been disciplined, my visual tastes have actually changed.

I'm just not drawn to young babes as I once was, and that's surprising, especially considering the family I hail from. Even my eighty-something grandfather, years past his prime, was hanging posters of nude women around his apartment at his age. Perhaps that's why I thought I'd grow up to be a dirty old man to some degree. I thought every guy did.

But God has different plans for those who follow Him. If we walk in His truth and stay disciplined with our eyes, we will be ravished by the wife of our youth until the day we die. We shouldn't be resigned to becoming lecherous, dirty old men. God has something better waiting for us...a wonderful partner who, Lord willing, we can grow old with and who can continue to satisfy us—even into the golden years.

And He has one more command that will take us there. We are to go another step beyond training our eyes so that our tastes can change along with our wife's changing body. We are to look past her outer shell and gaze deeply upon her inner beauty as well. God wants our eyes to lock on to her inner beauty from the word *go*. Look at His command to our wives:

Your beauty should not come from outward adornment, such as braided hair and the wearing of gold jewelry and fine clothes. Instead, it should be that of your inner self, the unfading beauty of a gentle and quiet spirit, which is of great worth in God's sight. For this is the way the holy women of the past who

put their hope in God used to make themselves beautiful.
(1 Peter 3:3-5)

If God wants women to concentrate on their inner beauty, what do you suppose God wants us *men* to concentrate on in our wives and girlfriends? Answer: their inner beauty.

You see, I'm not having sex with the tent anymore (I'll explain myself in a second). I'm having sex with what's inside, her soul and spirit. Her tent, like mine, has fading glory:

> For while we are in this tent, we groan and are burdened, because
> we do not wish to be unclothed but to be clothed with our heav-
> enly dwelling, so that what is mortal may be swallowed up by life.
> (2 Corinthians 5:4)

Our bodies are just tents. Have you ever seen those one-man tube tents at the sporting-goods store? That's essentially what our bodies are. As men, we are not to be focused on tents or to be having sex with the tent alone. We are supposed to be having sex with the wonderful human soul lying inside.

Our culture's obsession with tents is like some bizarre Dr. Seuss verse:

> *Playboy* bewitches with tents in their foldouts,
> While *SI*'s new beach tents have led to their sold-outs.
> The tents that are buxom and slim become treasure,
> While those who are not do not give us much pleasure.

We're worse than those Sneetches with "stars upon thars"! Twice as arrogant and three times as selfish, we are far less than normal in the way we see women. Christ, our standard for normal, looked past the tent and into the heart.

I've rejected this strange, obsessive tent world. When I look at Brenda, I don't see her tent anymore. I see her.

Oh sure, Fred.

It's true, and I respond by quoting Paul again:

I am telling the truth in Christ, I am not lying, my conscience testifies with me in the Holy Spirit. (Romans 9:1, NASB)

Why does this surprise you? That's a pop quiz in its own right and worthy of a deep look inside. Are you obsessed with her tent, obsessed with her weight and cup size? Who has bewitched you along the way?

My wife is more sensual to me today than she's ever been in my life because I'm no longer having sex with her tent alone. I'm meeting up with that lovely, ravishing woman inside with the "unfading beauty of a gentle and quiet spirit."

Reject your obsession with tents! The glory of her tent *will* fade, and her walls will stretch and bag with time, but her sensuality and your passion need never fade.

Quiz

Do your eyes look critically at your wife's body, or have they been transformed to gaze inside at her stunning beauty?

Do you believe it's possible to cherish the wife of your youth always, even into old age? Don't you believe that God's Word is for you?

spiritual intimacy blooms

How important is a prayer life with your wife? Some pastors say, in so many words, "Don't sweat it! The key to a good marriage rests in *your* having a vibrant personal prayer life with God. Praying with your wife is frosting on the cake but not really necessary."

While you may be surprised to hear me say this, I must be honest and say I recognize some truth in that philosophy. I lived that way for many years, and our marriage grew quite well.

But let's get even more honest. For most of us the real reason we don't consistently pray with our wives has nothing to do with some well-thought-out spiritual philosophy we've used to dismiss the need. Rather, most of us have simply never tried, and many who did have simply quit in frustration.

Maybe those few times you prayed together were too dry and boring, or maybe it was good for one of you but not for the other. Then the kids came along and wrung away more and more time. Maybe your sexual sin made you feel far too guilty to walk in the garden of prayer with your pure wife. So you threw in the towel, dismissing prayer and salving your conscience by convincing yourself that it was unimportant anyway.

But your prayer life together *is* important. Sure, you might be able to have a good marriage without it, but that misses the point entirely.

The real question here is this: *Can my marriage meet God's call without shared prayer?* If you think it can, then you have another thing coming to you. You won't be able to become truly one without it, and unless you become one with her, you've missed His highest call for your life together as a couple.

Besides, you need a tight prayer life for the protection it brings to your marriage. Not only does the deep intimacy of marital prayer rival the vibrant excitement of sexual intimacy, but it can easily anchor your victory over sexual sin, which should be a high priority for you on this side of purity.

Sin had placed a wall between Brenda and me in the spirit realm. The same wall stands (or once stood) between you and your wife, just as God said it would:

> Husbands, in the same way be considerate as you live with your
> wives, and treat them with respect as the weaker partner and as heirs
> with you of the gracious gift of life, so that nothing will hinder your
> prayers. (1 Peter 3:7)

Fantasizing over some buxom actress from *Baywatch* reruns is adultery. Do you suppose adultery is being considerate to your wife? She may not even know about your sin, but there are no secrets in God's realm. Sexual sin hinders your prayer life around the clock.

Even if you could ignore the fact that your prayers are hindered, there's still no ignoring your guilt. I'll never forget the time when my friend Tim discussed this subject with me. First, he opened a Bible and read 1 Corinthians 5:11:

> But now I am writing you that you must not associate with anyone
> who calls himself a brother but is sexually immoral or greedy, an idola-

ter or a slanderer, a drunkard or a swindler. With such a man do not even eat.

Tim looked at me, and what he said next was brutally honest: "I could not stand praying with Cindy back when I was masturbating. I always felt so creepy. I mean, after all, the Bible tells her not to even *associate* with a sexually immoral person. Yes, that meant me, the one masturbating behind her back. In a real sense, she wasn't even supposed to eat a meal with me, yet I was conveniently hiding my sin and expecting her to have sex with me."

Sound familiar? It does to me. I, too, avoided prayer because of my guilt over sexual sin. I rationalized it away because of my "star status" at church as a teacher and lay leader. *I'm at least as good as everyone else around here! Besides,* I figured, *what's the difference? God's sovereign! He's going to do what He's going to do whether I pray with Brenda or not, so no harm's done.*

But there *was* much harm done. I needed a prayer life with my wife, and so do you.

Of course, there are many obstacles to prayer with your spouse. While sexual sin is a big obstacle, it is not the only one. Because of that, eliminating sexual sin alone won't naturally birth a vibrant prayer life with your wife. You must still deal with the other obstacles.

That being said, building a prayer life on this side of purity will be a lot easier than it was on the other side, now that you have that hindrance and guilt out of the way. You can approach prayer more honestly and focus more deeply on the other obstacles, blowing past them in due time.

Do you believe that prayer times with your wife can be so intimate that they rock your emotions and passions as deeply as sex?

If you answered no, then your prayer life is stunted. You can go much deeper.

Intrigued? You should be. Take it from me, it is well worth the effort to get there.

anchoring our victory

The LORD accepts my prayer.

PSALM 6:9

When Dale attended a large men's conference a few years ago, one of the speakers prompted him to write out his testimony and declare that Jesus Christ was the Lord of his life.

I bumped into Dale recently, and we talked about that weekend. "You remember that testimony I wrote a couple of years ago?" he said. "I cannot make the same claim with any real validity today. I've become a total slave to pornography again. I feel so utterly humiliated! I don't know how I could let this happen… Well, that really isn't true. I know exactly how. I've fallen far away from the deep intimacy I once had with Jesus."

Poor Dale. I felt for him because worship and prayer must be life and death to us in this battle. We must seek Him with all our heart.

What is prayer like on the other side of victory over sexual impurity? Even though I've lived through this kind of restoration myself, I was enthralled to hear another story, this time from a fellow named Garrett.

"You wouldn't believe it!" he exclaimed. "I'd been in ministerial studies for a year and a half already, so you have to know that I was reading my Bible plenty. I was praying a lot too. But when I started bouncing my eyes, and the lust rolled away, it was as if the Bible opened up like a blue sky after a really dark night. Bouncing my eyes really helped me read my Bible better.

"But I've noticed an interesting thing: When I read my Bible less and don't stay close to the Word, it's harder to bounce my eyes. They really go hand in hand, and one can't be done very well without the other.

"And another thing. I used to get lustful thoughts popping up all the time during prayer. But now that my eyes are protected, it doesn't happen, so my prayer time has become much deeper and uninterrupted. Worshiping God is better as well. Now I feel free to express my heart to God."

That was the first change I noticed in my prayer life too: the focus and the peace. My flesh had been like a rabid crowd tossing rocks and clods over my prayer walls to distract me and draw me out. Rooting out the sexual sin dispersed the crowd, and over time I could feel how my relationship with the Lord was becoming profoundly deeper.

As it did, my prayer life changed yet again. So often in the past I'd felt unworthy to be heard because of my sin. And I'd often mumble and whine in tears and discouragement, hoping God might find it in His heart to listen if I could only make Him feel sorry for me.

But that's changed. Today, I feel like His son and can see myself through His eyes. I am His *son!* I'm always worthy to be heard, no matter what time of day. He simply loves me to death, just as He loves you. Maybe this story will illustrate just how He feels toward you and your prayers.

My thirteen-year-old son Jasen had been in school all day, which was followed by a hot, dismal football practice. I took the family to Pizza Hut for dinner, but awaiting Jasen at home afterward was a lousy load of homework.

As we got out of the car and headed inside, Jasen's face crumpled a bit. "Dad, I've had a really bad day," he said.

"What's the matter, Son?"

He glanced around to see if any of his siblings were listening. Knowing that he wanted a little privacy, I said, "Hey, let's get on up to your bedroom and talk about it."

In his room, he sprawled backward on the bed in an odd, discouraged way. It hurt me to see him like that.

"Sit up, Son," I coached him. "You'll feel better and besides, I need to hear you face to face. Now tell me all about it."

He began to unload his issues, but he mumbled his words, which made it sound like he was whining. Twice I stopped him and asked him to start over. After whining a *third* time, I said, "Jasen. Stop. You are my *son*. I'm your *dad*. Just tell me in your normal voice so I can hear."

I wanted so badly to convey a message to my precious boy: *You are my son. You don't need a shrill whine to convince me that your feelings are worthy enough for me to care about. I cared from the moment you brought it up. I love you!*

And your Father loves you. You are His son, and all your concerns are worthy. Lift up your head and, in your normal voice, go deep with God in prayer. As you do, this weighty new intimacy will anchor your victory over sexual sin.

Quiz

Has the anchor of prayer formed in your life?

Do you know He cares from the beginning when you
  address Him?

prayer's starting gun

My son, if you accept my words and store up my commands within you…then you will understand the fear of the LORD and find the knowledge of God. . . . Then you will understand what is right and just and fair—every good path.

PROVERBS 2:1,5,9

As a Christian, it's what you pray, not what you do.

These are great words—words I'd both loved and ignored for many years until I decided it was time to get with the program…God's program. But how? I'd never had a regular prayer life before, and while I had some ideas scrounged from a few sermons along the way, I knew I'd be flying blind. So I hesitated, pondering and stewing about what to do next to become a man of prayer.

Then an idea popped into my head as I mulled over a recent battle with sexual sin. What if I just obeyed and got started? Maybe God will teach me as I go.

During that battle I had learned that obedience is the starting pistol of change in God's kingdom. You may recall how I was originally challenged by Job's startling declaration in Job 31:1: "I made a covenant with my eyes not to look lustfully at a girl."

But while I was challenged, nothing changed. When I first gave serious consideration to Job's example, all I could do was meditate upon his words for days because I didn't know how to do this covenant thing. Oh sure, I could say the words to make a promise, but I was uncertain whether I could keep my word.

As for my eyes, that was even worse. Could I really expect my eyes to keep their end of the bargain? Eyes can't think or talk! How do they keep a promise?

Clearly, a challenge alone is not a starting gun. Though Job's words had challenged me, my eyes kept locking in on the figures of just about every female who stepped in front of my gaze. While I was deliberating over Job's words day and night, my eyes didn't change their ways, and my understanding grew little.

But I do remember the exact moment that turned out to be the crack of the starting pistol. I'd just failed God with my eyes for the thirty millionth time. My heart churned in guilt, pain, and sorrow. Driving down Merle Hay Road in Des Moines, I suddenly gripped the wheel and through clenched teeth yelled out: "That's it! I'm through with this! I'm making a covenant with my eyes. I don't care what it takes, and I don't care if I die trying. It stops here. It stops here!"

I began obeying in that instant. I didn't know anything more about covenants than I did the moment before, but I was off and running. Each time I averted my eyes, I ran another long stride down the obedience track.

Then I read something that Oswald Chambers wrote in *My Utmost for His Highest* (October 10 entry) that really put it together for me:

All of God's revealed truths are sealed until they are opened to us through obedience. You will never open them through philosophy or thinking. But once you obey, a flash of light comes immediately. If you obey God in the first thing He shows you, then He instantly opens up the next truth to you.

I *was* obeying God in the first thing He showed me…bouncing my eyes from joggers and sexy-dressed women. He suggested that be my first step, reminding me of what I'd read at Stanford years ago, that a man can draw sexual gratification through his eyes.

Having confronted the problem with my *eyes,* I turned my attention to my mind. Stepping out once more in obedience, I confronted my *thoughts* about my ex-girlfriend Polly. Again the Lord faithfully opened the next truth, teaching me through His Word that it's possible to take any thought captive that opposes His purposes for me as a Christian husband. And I obeyed.

On another occasion I took another step of obedience and committed my life to God's purposes in my marriage, no matter how painful and no matter how much gravel I had to eat. As I did so, He opened yet another truth. He let me know that Brenda would become all I'd ever dreamed about if I'd just cherish her, even when I didn't feel like it. *Right feelings always follow right actions,* He mentioned. *Besides, women are responders, and Brenda is no different.* In these three examples from my own life, I could see clearly that Oswald Chambers was right—a step of obedience *does* open the next truth.

So now I stood at the threshold of a fresh new frontier—regular prayer. I'd been sitting around meditating about prayer and pondering what to do next but getting nowhere. I only whined to myself, *What's my problem?*

But now as I reflected on my recent experience with sexual sin, my problem seemed clear. Looking back, I realized that I could have philosophized and meditated about my eyes and covenants until the cows came home, but I never would have learned a thing until I stepped out in obedience.

I sensed it would be the same with prayer. So I just started and counted on God to open the truths as I ran forward. I looked up some scriptures to get a feel for the things God asks us to pray for. Then I made up a prayer list for each day of the week. On Thursdays, for instance, I prayed for my lost relatives, my lost friends, and missionaries. On Fridays I prayed for my enemies, including my business competition and people who had recently hurt me.

It wasn't long, however, before the daily routine of prayer began to irk me. I heard my flesh say to me, "Look at that stinking list! Day after day you go to your list and pray the same old things. What a drag! You're just wasting your time and boring God silly." Funny, but I thought I could hear Satan's echo in there somewhere too. My heart began to fail in its commitment, and my flesh began stinking things up like a three-day-old mackerel.

But I obeyed, and God was about to open the next truth. One morning I honestly prayed, "Lord, is this really a waste of time? If I'm off track, just tell me what to do next. Am I boring You with my many words? I really want to know what to do."

To my utter amazement, Hebrews 9:6 instantly popped into my head. *What's up with that?* I had no idea what that particular scripture said. I scurried to my Bible and opened it up:

> When everything had been arranged like this, the priests entered regularly into the outer room to carry on their ministry. (Hebrews 9:6)

As I read the words, the Holy Spirit expanded its meaning by saying, *It has always been My plan that My children discipline themselves daily to come to Me, and it's okay to do the same things over and over. You are doing fine.*

Relieved, I murmured to myself, "Oh, okay, I get it. Good." Then suddenly it hit me. "God just gave me a Bible verse! We're talking!" God had revealed one more truth as I took one more step of obedience. That got me bouncing off the ceiling, and I had no trouble praying each morning for quite a while after that.

But eventually, I sensed something was missing. So I asked the Lord, "Isn't there more to all this than grinding through a list? I don't feel like I'm getting any closer to you, Lord."

It wasn't long before I heard Charles Swindoll mention on his *Insight for Living* radio broadcast that he never enters prayer without first entering worship—singing or humming a few songs to himself. That's the ticket! I started there by memorizing a few choruses to some popular worship songs from church. I especially liked the love songs that told Jesus how much I loved Him. One of my favorites today begins with this lyric: "You're the One that I love." Another starts with "I will worship You, my Love."

As I sang each morning, I reminded myself that the Lord loves to hear love songs sung to Him and that obedience is the key that opens every door, though at first the singing felt odd to me. It wasn't long before I found these songs were opening my heart to deeper prayer. Once again, another truth was opened as I obeyed.

A reader recently asked me, "What does intimacy with God look like? I know in my heart that it is true that there is a romance side to it, but that seems weird, and I can't get my head around that. But until I do, how can I get immersed in Him?"

You don't have to get your head around it, and there is nothing weird about it once you're there. You just need to get started. Your obedience will open the truths as you go.

Quiz

Is prayer still a mystery?
Have you fired the starting gun of obedience?
Just when are you going to become a man of prayer?

the ten prayer chillers I

For wisdom will enter your heart, and knowledge will be pleasant to your soul. Discretion will protect you, and understanding will guard you.

PROVERBS 2:10-11

Near my six-week mark of going cold turkey by denying the lust of my eyes, I had a very sensual and violent dream. I remember being sexually tempted in an extremely enticing manner and yet, for the first time in a dream, actually saying, "No, I won't." (You'll know you're nearing victory when, even in the freedom of your dreams, your subconscious mind chooses purity.) This statement caused violent, hand-to-hand combat to ensue, and I cried out, "In the name of Jesus, I will defeat you!"

When I said the words, "In the name of Jesus," the battle turned in my favor. Confident that victory was at hand, I declared, "I will defeat you"—at which point the battle turned violently against me. I forgot that I had no power of my own—but she didn't—and that gave her an opening to attack. In desperation, I cried out every name of Jesus I could think of.

Suddenly I awoke with a start, praising God spontaneously and uncontrollably in victory. It was Sunday morning.

Several hours later, in church, I worshiped freely for the first time. Praises continued to percolate from my heart the rest of the day, that night, and into the next day. For someone who had felt such distance from God for so long, the feeling was glorious. Better yet, that freedom to worship has remained to this day.

But one thing that didn't click was feeling comfortable enough to pray with Brenda. For years I had avoided prayer with Brenda because of my sexual sin. After this breakthrough worship, I assumed that our prayer life would spontaneously blossom in the same way. It didn't, so I began searching my heart: *Why don't I have a vibrant prayer life with my wife?*

I wanted to end each day in the bedroom together, holding hands and lifting up our marriage, our children, and our needs to God. But doing that felt strange to me, partly because I had never done it before. On top of that, if we happened to be intimate afterward, that could *really* feel strange.

Perhaps you feel the same way. Why are we men like this? What is it about praying with our wives that's so unnatural, so…intimidating? It's because there are Prayer Chillers out there, similar to the ten Love Chillers that Steve and I introduced in *Every Man's Marriage.* Let's take a closer look at why we have such a tough time praying with our loved ones:

1. Men are rebellious by nature. We get bored fast with the straight life. We'd rather do things our way or the easy way, and that includes bailing out on the discipline of prayer. In many ways, I was too lazy to get with the prayer program with Brenda. My rationalization could be summed up in this way: "Who cares? Brenda and I are doing fine as it is. It's such a time hog, so why push on this prayer thing? That's just legalistic hash these pastors are dishing out."

2. The male ego is bigger but more fragile than the female ego. We must have fragile egos, because most men would rather sit in a dentist's chair than pray with their wives. I had been a Christian for exactly one year when I met Brenda, who had grown up from the cradle in the church. She knew it all—and I didn't. I knew nothing about leading a home spiritually, but I was sensitive about admitting this to Brenda. When my lack of competence showed, I usually got angry. My male ego couldn't handle my inadequacy, and it was often easier to slough off praying together than to risk taking leadership and acting like a rookie.

Still, I can remember screwing up the courage to attempt to pray with Brenda a number of times under some new plan I'd recently devised. But it usually ended up in the same dust heap a few days later. I'd fumble and bumble my way through the experience, almost feeling my wife mentally rolling her eyes. Then I'd get mad because she wasn't being open to my leadership.

Our first plan was to pray as she was used to praying. That meant I would pray a short prayer of everything I could think of before turning the floor over to Brenda, who would pray for a *much* longer time as she recounted everything she could think of. After a while I found this droning method formal and stifling, and in typical male fashion, I informed Brenda about my feelings.

Going to Plan B, I suggested we try something that I had learned in a men's group that was called the Ping-Pong method. Under this scenario, each person simply prays for one or two things before yielding the floor to someone else to pray. Then you bounced back and forth until you were finished. I liked this open-ended approach because I thought it would add life and interaction to our prayer times together.

Brenda agreed to try my new plan, but she didn't put her heart into it. After all, she'd been a Christian a long time and liked her way of praying quite well. Anyway, after a mere two sessions she snorted, "I hate this Ping-Pong thing. When you are praying I never know if I'm supposed to be agreeing with you in prayer or praying for my own stuff silently or just what I'm supposed to do. It all seems disjointed and bizarre to me."

That attitude set me off. "Why can't you ever just follow my lead and help me out some?" I snapped. "You always have to have it your way! Who do you think you are, God's guru or something?"

That was my ego talking, and you can imagine how our prayer relationship got placed in a deep freezer for many months after that outburst.

3. Men are relatively less sensitive to the needs of others. In a perfect world, the head of the home would be the most sensitive one in the house. But we don't live in a perfect world!

I always prayed on my knees or while pacing back and forth. I always felt that a respectful posture from Brenda was very important to God and an encouragement to me.

I was appalled the first time I prayed with Brenda! She just laid back casually against the headboard on the bed! I said, "Brenda! C'mon, we're praying, not counting sheep! I can't pray if you are going to lie around like that! 'Hey, everyone, look at how much Brenda cares about prayer!' Brother!"

That was certainly insensitive of me to say that. If I had respectfully inquired why Brenda lay in bed to pray with me, she would have told me that she doesn't like to pace when she prays, because she can't concentrate when she does it. And if she kneels next to the bed and lays her head across her arms, for some reason that just knocks her out and she falls asleep in a flash.

My insensitivity inhibited our prayer life from growing. What about you? Have you made any insensitive comments in this area?

We'll discuss the remaining seven Prayer Chillers in our next chapter.

Quiz

Do you recognize yourself in the Prayer Chillers list?
Specifically, which chillers are trampling your prayer life with
  your wife?

the ten prayer chillers II

A wise man has great power, and a man of knowledge increases strength.

PROVERBS 24:5

Let's pick up where we left off in the previous chapter:

4. *Men are less able to express emotions and feelings verbally than women.* Of course, the corollary is that women are *very* able to express themselves verbally. Praying with Brenda drove me crazy! When it was her turn to pray, she'd go on and on and on and on about everything—from the sore toe bothering Peaches, her mother's dog, to her great-aunt Hattie's indigestion. Ugh. If my blood pressure wasn't soaring from the endless tedium, my eyes were blinking back the deep sleep of indifference.

5. *The male brain is more oriented to facts and logic than emotions and intuitions.* Because of brain differentiation during fetal development, the male brain has fewer lateral transmission points between its two hemispheres. With this bent toward facts and logic, we're more apt to desire a quick and methodical trip down our list than a deep, searching, yearning prayer time focused on the needs of our family. This doesn't exactly lend itself to vibrancy in prayer.

6. *Men are sexually stimulated visually.* Your heart may be set to lead your wife into prayer as you lie on your bed, waiting on her to join you.

Then she slips off her jeans and T-shirt and stands there in her bra and panties. Throwing on her nightgown, she then reaches behind her back to unsnap her bra, which she casually tosses aside. Your mind races.

Then, while she brushes her teeth, she bends over just enough… Mission Control drones, "We have ignition," and now your mind is on only one thing.

Sex can really get in the way of prayer for guys. As Ed says, "For me, I find myself asking, 'Is this a sex night or a prayer night?' It's always an either/or because it feels funny to have sex after praying. I also find it positively impossible to pray *after* making love."

7. *During courtship, males will initiate the prayer relationship—but after the wedding things are different.* Before there's a wedding band on her finger, we run two steps ahead to open doors or listen intently as she describes her hopes for raising a big family. We do this because we want to win her heart. Things often change after the wedding, however. Guys aren't as interested in hearing *everything* she has to say or in having that prayer time together. Again, it often has something to do with wanting to get to bed.

Having put our best foot forward to conquer the love frontier, we turn the reins of the spiritual relationship over to our wives and climb back into our Conestoga wagon for a nap.

8. *Men need less romance and intimacy than women.* The intense intimacy of prayer can freeze even the best of us. One time we invited Tom Treynor and his wife, Angie, to our home. Tom had grown up as a missionary kid and was serving in the Middle East. He and Angie were the first missionary couple we'd put up in our home during our church's annual missions convention, and we were pumped. Tom and Angie were about our age, newly married, and absolutely bubbling over with a passion for Christ's call on their life.

But I'll never forget Tom's words as we discussed the struggle of building a prayer life as a young couple: "Prayer with your wife is just so intimate. It's harder than standing naked in front of a stranger!"

9. *The male shield from feeling inferior is his work.* The wife's shield from

feeling inferior is generally her husband, so she naturally places a higher value on the relational aspect of prayer than her husband does. Spiritual oneness may not even be on his radar screen. But his work will be!

I can't tell you how many times I've blown off prayer after 10:00 p.m., saying, "It's just too late, sweetheart! I've got to get my sleep because of that early appointment tomorrow." When we continually break appointments with God and our wives to make appointments with others, a vibrant prayer life is just a misty dream.

10. Men desire peace from marriage; women desire oneness and intimacy. We can easily be satisfied with a "business partner" relationship in marriage as long as there's peace and enough sex. That applies to our prayer lives as well. Early in our marriage, after a long day of raising toddlers and working at the office, Brenda and I would jump into prayer without stopping to catch our breath. Like good little people, we came together, did our prayer duty, and called it a day…steady and ordered. Peaceful.

Maybe too peaceful. Looking back, I wish we'd had a better sense of what we wanted to accomplish when we prayed, and I wish we had spent a little more time sharing our hearts before we began each night. Maybe we would have gotten more out of it.

Well, there you have it, the ten Prayer Chillers. They don't form the most encouraging list, do they? By nature, men are insensitive, poorly focused, and have little interest in praying with their wives. No wonder vibrant prayer is so rare between a married couple. That's too bad, because today I realize that there is nothing that Brenda and I do that binds us more tightly as a couple. Your marriage needs this—much more than you know.

Quiz

Do you pray often with your wife?

Have obstacles rendered your joint prayer life common and ordinary?

when prayer became good

Pray continually…for this is God's will for you in Christ Jesus.
1 THESSALONIANS 5:17-18

When my prayer life with Brenda didn't blossom naturally after my victory over sexual sin, I pretty much gave up on it. You could say that the Prayer Chillers made me feel like the first settler crossing the Rocky Mountains. I'd scaled the first mountain of sexual sin to the summit only to find the Prayer Chiller Range stretching as far as I could see to the west. Other obstacles poked skyward as well. When Brenda's father, Frank, was diagnosed with colon cancer when she was eighteen, she valiantly and fiercely prayed for his healing. After two long, painful years, however, she lost her treasured father, and for the next ten years Brenda barely believed in the power of prayer.

Interestingly, the success of our marriage became an obstacle to prayer too. Yes, I said *success.* I've already mentioned that our marriage was in a shambles early on, but when things turned around, our relationship was humming so well that we were asked to teach premarriage and marriage classes on Wednesday evenings at church. Who needed prayer together? Love and commitment were getting us through. I was finally treating her with respect, and our intimacy was blooming. If our prayer life together never blossomed along with it, so what? I figured I was grading out pretty well in Marriage 101.

But then evangelist Rich Wilkerson buzzed through town one day and delivered a pop quiz that sent my grades reeling. "In the early years of traveling about in our ministry, my wife, Robin, and I would stay in the oldest run-down, no-tell motels. That's all we could afford. We had nothing but a call to preach God's love to kids.

"I would get up early in the morning every day to go out and start knocking on the doors of the public schools for several hours in hope of getting the opportunity to teach our message of love. As I would leave each morning, Robin would slip out of bed and go to her knees on those gross, grungy carpets. Then she'd pray and ask God to open doors for me while I was gone.

"Often, I'd fumble with my keys through my tears as I tried to start my car after walking out that door, knowing she was already in there battling for me. Many times I'd return and there she'd be, still on her knees on that dirty carpet. She was so brave, so steadfast, and so loving to me. What a warrior!"

Would Brenda or I pray with our knees in the dirt for our Wednesday-night classes? I couldn't even imagine it. Not only had I scored a zero on this pop quiz, it was as though I'd never even cracked a textbook—I couldn't even relate to the material. Then I read this scripture:

You say, "I am rich; I have acquired wealth and do not need a thing." But you do not realize that you are wretched, pitiful, poor, blind and naked. (Revelation 3:17)

Never did I find myself more convicted by Scripture than at this moment. I thought we had a lot going, but in a deeper sense, we really didn't. I was missing out on a whole field of intimacy with Brenda that I didn't even know existed.

To my shame, for years nothing really changed regarding our prayer life together. Still, Rich Wilkerson's story caused me to think, and it altered the way I viewed prayer forever. I never minimized it again.

So when *did* prayer finally become good for us? It's a long and winding story, but in a single sentence: Prayer became good when we gave worship a big promotion and sex a proper demotion.

Taking that first step should have been a no-brainer, since I'd been using worship in my own prayer times for years, but I'd never considered bringing my boom box and CDs into prayer with Brenda. Remember, prayer with your wife is already as intimate as standing naked in front of a stranger—and who wants to stand naked *and* sing in front of a stranger?

But almost by accident, we began worshiping together as a couple. When we did, our prayer life together simply exploded in intimacy.

How do we go about it? There is nothing to it, really. Brenda sits in the lounger in a corner of the bedroom while I pace in the opposite corner. Turning on a CD of quiet worship songs, we both begin to sing and pray quietly and independently to the Lord.

Opposite corners? What's so intimate about that? Nothing, at first. But the key to our intimacy together is making an intimate connection with Christ first, on our own, before coming together in prayer.

While playing two or three songs, Brenda sits with the Lord, worshiping Him, just the two of them. I make the same connection with Him in the other corner, and then, when I sense the moment is right, I bring us together in the center of the room.

Turning the music low, Brenda and I come together face to face, maybe a foot apart, and hold hands. She bows her head a little while I raise mine, and we begin to pray.

Nothing I've ever experienced beats the electricity of these moments together—the touch, the passion, the tears. It has all the fiery intimacy of sex with none of the sensuality or self-focus. Our hearts become one in Him, and nothing else matters but the three of us.

The Prayer Chillers evaporate in the warm glow of these intimate moments. For instance, I don't mind how long she prays, and fighting off sleep is the furthest thing from my mind. I don't even mind if she prays for her mom's dog. My ego disappears, and it doesn't matter if she can pray better than I can or if she's had more experience. Since I've already connected with the Lord before coming together with her, my agendas seem pointless. Putting worship in its place has been the key to prayer intimacy in our bedroom.

Now let's take a closer look at how prayer jells with the sexual relationship. Putting sex in its place was just as vital for Brenda and me. Scripture reminds us that prayer always has the preeminent place over sex in a normal marriage relationship:

> The wife's body does not belong to her alone but also to her husband. In the same way, the husband's body does not belong to him alone but also to his wife. Do not deprive each other except by mutual consent and for a time, so that you may devote yourselves to prayer. Then come together again so that Satan will not tempt you because of your lack of self-control. (1 Corinthians 7:4-5)

I think it's safe to say that most guys are more interested in having sex than in having prayer with their wives, so most of us tip this verse on its ear and work things in reverse. Rather than deprive ourselves of sex for the sake of prayer, we deprive ourselves of prayer before bed so that we might devote our time to sex.

Our victory over sexual sin helps us turn things right side up again, and not just by keeping sexual thoughts from racing around our heads while we pray. Our new control over our appetites and desires enables us to delay sexual gratification and to put sex in its proper place in relation to prayer.

If there are never times when you desire prayer with your wife more than you desire sex with her, then your prayer life is on life support and your life is out of balance. At one time, I *always* chose sex over prayer, and then the Holy Spirit delivered yet another pop quiz to my desk.

A friend of mine was struggling to find time to read his Bible every morning, but he noticed he always found the time to read the morning paper. So, he made a rule that he couldn't read the morning newspaper until he had first read the Bible. I was proud of him, and I loved this rule. *What a great idea!* I thought. Until the Holy Spirit took and applied that idea to *my* life, whispering, *It is a great idea, isn't it? Now, why not put it to use in your life?*

What do you mean, Lord? I asked in my heart. *I already have my mornings with You under control!*

I knew He was grinning when He said, *Ah, but what about your nights?*

Oops. I got it. I couldn't quite find the time I needed for prayer with Brenda, but I always seemed to squeeze in time for sex. Since sex was pushing out my prayer time with Brenda, I felt the Holy Spirit was suggesting that I make a rule like my friend did with the newspaper. So I decided that, for a time, I would no longer make love with Brenda unless we first had a time of prayer together. I wanted to break some bad habits in me and learn to prioritize prayer a little better. Brenda agreed to go along with my plan for a while.

Nothing I've done as a spiritual discipline was tougher than that. Sometimes we only had time for one or the other, so we chose prayer and missed out on sex entirely. Sometimes I was simply infuriated at the rule as my passions bubbled. But after a number of months, prayer with Brenda became so intimate and so special that for the first time in my life, I began to prefer prayer over sex on a fairly regular basis.

It was then that our prayer life became really, really good for us.

Quiz

Does your desire for the intimacy of prayer with your wife
ever trump your desire for sexual intimacy?

If a joint prayer life hasn't blossomed naturally for you, what
is God calling you to do about it? Isn't it time to get with
it...fish or cut bait?

a band of brothers going awol

Revive us, and we will call on your name.

PSALM 80:18

As head of the intercession group at my church a few years ago, I co-founded a weekly citywide meeting to pray for revival in Des Moines. One pastor, despondent over the lack of men showing up, asked me to challenge his men's group one Wednesday night. I had prayed with the Tuesday-night intercession group many times, but those ranks were filled mostly with women.

Stepping up to the podium, I declared, "There's something wrong on Tuesday nights. Whenever Brenda and I show up to pray for our city, my wife can look up for encouragement and find sisters standing shoulder to shoulder with her in the battle. When I look up, however, I can only ask, 'Where are my brothers?'"

The room became still. Then I read the following scripture:

And He looked up and saw the rich putting their gifts into the treasury. And He saw a poor widow putting in two small copper coins. And He said, "Truly I say to you, this poor widow put in more than all of them; for they all out of their surplus put into the offering; but she out of her poverty put in all that she had to live on." (Luke 21:1-4, NASB)

I could tell I had everyone's attention. "These men gave only out of their surplus," I continued, "yet this poor woman gave everything she had. You come to this men's group on Wednesday nights because it's easy—and you get to see your friends. As for the Tuesday-night prayer group, it's 'Oh, but I can't come. That will cost me family time!' Have your kids ever seen you fight for anything greater than your family time? Will they ever see a heroic father fight costly battles for Christ's glory in prayer? Or will you only give Him a pittance of your time?"

Drawing on a bit of history from their pastor, I continued, "You had a week of prayer services here last January. Out of two thousand people, thirty-four were on hand the first night, a Monday. By Thursday, you could only muster seventeen, and half of those were staff members required to attend."

Let's freeze frame my talk to the men's group for a moment and think about Jesus. On the darkest, most bitter night of His life, Jesus couldn't even get His best friends to pray:

Then He came to the disciples and found them asleep and said to Peter, "What, could you not watch with Me one hour?" (Matthew 26:40, NKJV)

Christ aches for the lost and yearns to bless His church. He longs for us to pray for salvation and revival, the passions of His heart. Have you spent even a *quarter* hour this week praying for the things on God's heart? Men throughout history have done far more.

For some years Rev. Andrew Murray Sr. spent several hours praying every Friday night for revival in South Africa. As a boy of thirteen, Evan

Roberts began to hunger, thirst, and pray for God to send revival to Wales. In the island village of Barvas, off the northwest coast of Scotland, seven young men entered into a covenant with God to gather three nights a week in a barn just outside town to pray for revival. All saw their prayers gloriously answered and the desires of God's heart fulfilled.

Will we only give God the things that cost us nothing? David refused to do so. How about us?

> But King David replied to Araunah, "No, I insist on paying the full price. I will not...sacrifice a burnt offering that costs me nothing."
> (1 Chronicles 21:24)

It doesn't cost much to become part of a men's group. We get cool shirts and ball caps and become part of a big brotherhood. We listen to wonderful speakers about how we can have better families and better sex lives. Tough duty!

But it costs plenty to pray with others. Prayer is hard work, and it takes courage, dedication, concentration, and steadfastness. Still, these are traits wired into us as men. We can answer God's call here, and we must! I know I've sensed God's heart calling to me, *You fill My altars with tears when your heart is breaking, but what of the things that break My heart? When I ask you to give up a little of your family time for prayer, you run!*

As I continued my talk to the men's group, I asked, "Can ten good men be found in this room to pray with the women on Tuesday nights? Are there not ten men who will come?"

There were one hundred in attendance that evening, so I thought asking for ten wasn't too much. In fact, I was embarrassed to ask for so few, but that was the number I felt the Lord had given me.

Even ten turned out to be a stretch. Only one man showed up at the Tuesday-night prayer meeting in the following weeks. It's hard to get men interested in the tough business of praying for those things on God's heart, like salvation and revival.

Let's face it, it's even hard to get men concerned about the things on their *wife's* heart—present company included. Recently, Brenda shared something that she wrote in her journal back in 1990 that illustrates how I was just as asleep as Jesus' disciples were on the eve of His death:

> My life needs a lot of work. I especially want to grow more in prayer. Seems like I've sure had some tough days lately since making a bigger effort to read my Bible, pray, and read about prayer. Fred and I had a tough day of disagreement yesterday. I know the Lord needs to work in both of our lives. I'm really praying for wisdom in that area.

Where was I when she was this heavy in heart and fighting this battle all alone? AWOL. A week later she wrote:

> This has been another hard day. I need to pray more consistently and diligently. I need to treat others with kindness and love and to give of myself unselfishly. There seems to be so many needs for so many things…teach Sunday school, help at the book fair and the missions party…the list goes on and on until I just want to scream at people to leave me alone. I want to withdraw and not help with anything, but then I have a bad attitude when I *do* go ahead and do something. Where is the balance? I used to have as a gift from the Lord the ability to do for others in complete love without thinking of myself. Now that gift seems to have vanished. Lord, please help me to find it again.

Brenda never asked me, "Fred, will you pray for these things with me?" She likely never gave it a thought. And why should she? As a prayer partner,

I was AWOL—absent without a leave. But she fought on alone, writing one month later:

> This new prayer discipline is helping! The Lord is speaking to me more to help me during the day. The other day Rebecca was getting into things, and I felt myself beginning to lose patience (I didn't, though), when the Lord spoke to me and said, "Watch out—another one's coming." It was as if the devil had laid a trap for me, waiting to watch me lose my patience again. Within about two minutes, Laura caught her finger in the lid of the toilet and couldn't get it out. Normally, that would have been the breaking point, but since I'd been warned to watch out, I didn't lose my temper. Please, Lord, help me to continue to grow!

I wasn't there to celebrate with her because I wasn't there to pray with her. I didn't shoulder one load for her either.

Guys, isn't it time to shoulder our wife's load? And how about shouldering our Lord's passions in prayer, as well? Get concerned about the things on her heart and the pursuits of His heart. You are His warrior, and the prayer of a righteous man avails much (see James 5:16, NKJV).

Quiz

Is your heart breaking over the things that are breaking God's heart?

Have you shed tears in your concern?

you own the field

You, dear children, are from God and have overcome them, because the one who is in you is greater than the one who is in the world.

I JOHN 4:4

During my struggles with sexual sin, Brenda paid a price for my profligacy as well. On Sunday mornings she'd sometimes awake in tearful panic, scared out of her wits by the frightening dream she'd just had in which she was being chased by Satan. Each time this happened, I was already awake. In fact, I'd be comfortably ensconced downstairs in a lounger and calmly lusting over lingerie ads in the Sunday paper. Was my immorality causing spiritual protection to be taken away from her?

Jorge wrote me that his wife experienced the same type of horrible dreams. "My wife, Mimi, had a nightmare in which Satan attacked her by the throat, which scared the living daylights out of her," he said. "Looking back, we realize that these began right about the time I got hooked by pornography."

Make no mistake, your spiritual covering and protection over your marriage and family are compromised by sexual sin. You would be a fool to think that your sin has no effect in the spiritual realm. I used to think that, but not anymore. When my sexual sin was stopped in its tracks, Brenda's dreams stopped too.

When Satan had your number, he kicked you up and down the field at will. Like it or not, righteousness carries clout in the spirit realm, but because of your sexual impurity, your clout was negligible. Your sin drained you, and your faith was anemic. Your sin gave Satan the ability to overpower you as well as a serious home-field advantage over your life.

But now your victory over sexual sin has been established. It is time to start running roughshod through Satan's line.

When I played football, I always felt I owned the field, whether at home or away. I played as if the turf was mine, and I could go wherever I wanted. If anyone tried to stop me, he'd be fiercely punished with a lowered shoulder and driving legs.

I suppose you could have called it a quiet arrogance, but it was also a justified arrogance. I knew the sacrifices I'd made to get strong. I knew that I'd outworked everyone on the field during the months leading up to that Friday-night game. I promised myself that no single player could ever stop me—period.

My commitment was total. I said no when I was invited to the Saturday-night keggers, and I ate and slept right. I knew my game plan and my coach's instructions top to bottom. I belonged on that field, and that field belonged to me.

Trash talk couldn't touch me. Well, hardly. I'll never forget the trash talk I heard from Washington High's Darrell "The Mill" Miller when I was playing high-school quarterback. The guy was a brute, a defensive tackle who got into a three-point stance and shouted that henceforth he was about to separate my bleeping head from my bleeping torso. You catch my drift.

Darrell could intimidate me at times, but mostly I chuckled at his profane promises and ignored the blasts of steam blowing out of his nostrils in the chill autumn air. It was all show biz.

The real show plays at the point of impact, the collision of wills and power. The collision of sacrifices made throughout the years—my years of commitment meeting his years of commitment in a moment of time. At that instant, words meant nothing. Only the commitment that led to my strength, balance, and confidence mattered.

It's little different on the spiritual field of battle. Faith comes, in part, from the same things: your commitment and obedience to your Coach.

Don't get me wrong. All power rests in God, and all faith originates in Him too. But sin lengthens the shadows of doubt in your spirit and sabotages your faith. You *know* you don't own the field, and you fear the point of impact with the Enemy.

On top of that, Satan's trash talk *does* intimidate, because he knows your weak spots and constantly reminds you of how you've blown it and sinned in the past.

Satan talked trash to me, too, whenever I tried to get right with God concerning my sexual sin. He was the king of trash talk who tried to intimidate me around the clock. He'd sneer, "You're weak, Stoeker. I've heard you running your mouth. You told me to go…so make me! Show me what you've got!"

Only faith and power move Satan.

But now you've overcome your sin, and your commitment to purity is sure. God owns the field, which means *you* own the field. Things are different now. Satan's lies don't have the same zing. In fact, you're incredulous when he speaks at all, like a senior responding to a sophomore challenge in the locker room.

Satan's antics will remind you of Tom Archer, a teammate on my sophomore squad. One afternoon after practice, Tom smarted off to Mike Jenkins, a senior co-captain of the 4-A state champion Jefferson J-Hawks. Mike knew what to do.

Enlisting several of the guys, they jumped Tom and promptly taped him, wearing only his jockstrap, to a bench. Tom, a hairy guy, looked like a mummy, and I knew it would be no picnic peeling the white adhesive tape from his skin.

But to add insult to injury, Mike wiped a glob of Atomic Balm heating rub across Tom's genitals. While the seniors laughed their heads off, Mike thundered, "If anyone tries to help Tom before every senior has left this locker room, he'll get the same treatment." Then he and the rest of the seniors took their sweet time in the showers.

Satan has intimidated you for years, but the tables have turned. Have you noticed? If you've moved into purity, I know you sense that he can't push you around anymore. You know who you are and whose you are. You know you're walking purely, and you're not afraid.

You're a senior now, so act like it. Give Satan a tape job and apply a little Atomic Balm where it counts.

Feeling like a novice is no excuse to sleep at your post or to run from battle. Warfare is a normal part of a man's responsibility. Sure, when you were in sexual sin, you were in survival mode. But now you've fought your battle for purity and won. Now you can breathe freely again, and now you're free to face this new challenge. What is every man's challenge on the other side of purity? To get out of survival mode and to become a man of valor.

So stand up and be one. You own the field! Who is the devil to think he can come onto your field? Who is he to think he can come into your home? He's like a sophomore; he has no authority there!

Get after Satan. Get a holy arrogance about you! Don't you get incensed when you think about what Satan did to you all these years? Don't you get riled to see what he's doing to your friends? Give him some of his own medicine. You're an upperclassman in the Lord, and purity is now yours. You are truly an overcomer, and it is high time you make Satan pay.

Quiz

Are you still getting kicked around, or do you sense a deep
   confidence in the Lord as you walk in Him?

After all He's done for us, God's eyes still must hunt high and
   low for men who will stand in the gap and intercede for
   Him. Will you step up and be a man on His battlefield?

a fresh view of marriage

It's common for us to receive e-mails from men saying, "I've done every-thing you've taught me in *Every Man's Battle*. My love for my wife is off the scale, as is my desire for her. But she's not responding to me. What's wrong? How can I get my wife to desire me sexually?"

Simple—quit trampling her emotionally. For women, interpersonal, emotional intimacy and sexual desire are tightly tied together. As you have advanced in defeating your sexual sin with the Lord, you are naturally mov-ing toward deeper sexual intimacy with her. But perhaps you haven't yet adjusted your leadership style, which would allow her sexual feelings toward you to make a similar advance. It doesn't matter how sexually pure you are: If you are still trampling her essence—her beliefs, her intellect, her voice, and her role as helpmate—then you should humble yourself and make even more changes in the way you treat your wife. Your leadership style may be more suffocating than you've dreamed.

Gratefully, your battle with sexual sin has equipped you with the humility and heart to see the sanctity of marriage more broadly. Since the battle for purity has taught you that sex is not all about you, you're now realizing that marriage isn't all about you either.

Your battle for purity also taught you that you can have some serious blind spots regarding the effects of your behavior in the lives of those around you. Because of that, you should now be more humble and open to the possibility that you can have blind spots in other areas of your relationship with your wife and your children. You should be braver in making self-inspections and quicker to ask your wife for the truth and to listen to her views.

To accept Christ is to accept a call to constant and even cataclysmic change in who you are and in how you think and respond to those around you. To embrace Christ is to embrace inspection and change, to embrace renewal and transformation both humbly and dauntlessly. To embrace Christ is to embrace the idea that you are flawed and that these flaws are trampling your relationships with God and others.

Speaking of relationships, think back and try to remember a minute…what did you want out of marriage? What did you want it to look like? How did you want your marriage to be different from that of your parents?

I dreamed a lot about marriage and knew exactly what I wanted, and do you know what? God also wanted that for me, and He wants it for you. God is really into relationships. After all, it was for relationship that we were created in the first place. After that, the first thing He didn't like in His creation was a lack of relationship, and He fixed the situation with His favorite thing…a relationship (between Adam and Eve). Jesus' final prayer (see John 17) was about relationships, and His final word on marriage through Paul was that men ought to make the ultimate sacrifice of their lives for their marriage relationships, just as He sacrificed His life for His own relationship with His Bride.

God loves marriage for many reasons but especially for the picture it paints…the picture of Christ's love that your marriage paints for your children…the picture of Christ's sacrifice that it paints for the lost…the picture of Christ's commitment that will disciple the believers. I've been told that the picture painted by our marriage has encouraged other couples to greater love and sacrifice in their own marriages.

So let's return to our question: What did you want out of marriage? Has marriage delivered what you dreamed it would? Or have you just lowered your expectations, mumbling, "Well, that was unrealistic to expect those things I wanted. When I look around, I realize that peace is really the only thing I can honestly hope for."

Let me tell you something. You don't have a right to lower your expectations. You don't have a right to settle for mere peace or mediocrity, either.

You have a call—likely the most important call in your life—to oneness in marriage. A lot is riding on your response to this call. You also have a choice, a choice between self-discipline or self-regret. Will you embrace the hard work and self-discipline of change, or will you meander the wide, easy way to marital mediocrity? You have no out because there is no third option. You must choose one or the other. But before you choose, let me remind you that the pain of self-discipline lasts only a short time, while the pain of regret lasts the rest of your life.

You once had a call to sexual purity, and you stood up and got it done. Now it's time to stand up and get it done God's way in your marriage, too. Imagine what would happen if Christian men would rise and walk normally in marriage, in Christ. Wouldn't the whole world sit up and notice?

That is what God wants…a marriage in your home that will make the world sit up and notice Him and what a great Father He is. He wants you to paint that kind of picture with your marriage.

are you listening?

Standing at one end of the football stadium beneath a sparkling blue sky in Boulder, Colorado, author and speaker Gary Smalley declared, "There are two very damaging ingredients in Christian homes today. The first is the man who wants to have too much control. The second is the man who creates too much distance and doesn't want people close to him."

Are you listening? No, not to Gary Smalley—but to your wife! You could be one of these damaging ingredients. I was, and I didn't even know it. I loved to control yet bore an uncontrolled tongue, uncontrolled passions, and an uncontrolled temper.

You may be as abnormal as I was, as well as deaf to the verbal clues. Stop and think for a moment. Has your wife ever asked why you always have to have the last word? Do your arguments often leave her in tears of frustration as she deals with your controlling feints and darts? Maybe her sex drive has cooled considerably, or maybe you've even received a letter like the one Brett's wife sent him:

Too many times the kids and I have attempted to communicate with you, but we have not been able to complete the task with you. This is in no way intended to make you feel bad or to place blame on you. I want you to look at us and try to feel our pain. The children love you dearly, but they don't understand why you are angry so much. There have been many times they have come and asked me if they had done something to make you mad.

I have issues with Brett's communication style, just like Brenda once had with mine. He readily uses sarcasm, mockery, talking down, belittling, name-calling, and hurtful words when he is angry and frustrated with them. He loves to take her comments and turn them around to change the meaning of what she was trying to say. For instance, if she says, "It doesn't matter who is right or wrong," he'll say, "So you don't think it matters what is right or wrong?" This completely changes the conversation and steers things down a different track, taking the spotlight off him and putting it on his wife. Brett's wife had more to say in her letter:

You have difficulty controlling your anger and amplify insignificant things to create even more anger. You don't stick with the immediate issues, and you often bring up past issues to muddy the waters. You love to provoke others to anger with your intimidation and lengthy lectures. You force others to agree with you. You just love to control us, making us do things that don't appear to serve a purpose, like making us clean the driveway between thunderstorms. Your favorite lectures begin with "What have you done for me?" or "Look what I've done for you!"

You made the comment the other day that the kids "are too argu-mentative" and will "reap what they have sown." This is a true statement for all of us, but there may be an even more important question to ask: Are the kids reaping what *you* are sowing? I think that is what's happening here.

You are the man of the house and our leader. I have no hesitation in following your lead when it is given in love and compassion, but you should understand that this does not give you free reign to control or disregard our feelings.

I want my husband back. I want the man I married. I want the man who gave me no doubts that he desired me. Where did he go? I'm waiting for his return because I need him.

When I reached age thirty-five, the lack of my father's acceptance suddenly rocked me. This pain affected my relationship with my wife and kids, and I fell into harsh ways again. I was harsh in my tone, harsh in my words. Harsh, harsh, harsh. Brenda tried to explain away my behavior, but after a year she became frustrated. One day she told me, "All right, then! Fine. Just tell all of us how long you plan to stay like this so we can prepare for it!" Then she stormed out of the room.

I sat there speechless for quite some time. How long *was* I going to stay like this? Ten years? Why ten? Why not five? If I could decide to change at the end of five years, why not after one? And if after one, why not now?

After her single stiletto question to my heart, I knew it was time. Starting immediately, I found a counselor. Shortly afterward I attended a Promise Keepers conference in Boulder, Colorado. God spoke to me through Greg Laurie, the opening-night speaker, and revealed an aspect of His love for me that I'd never understood before.

Sitting that evening in the bleachers at the University of Colorado's Folsom Field, the pain from my dad began to dissipate, and that feeling continued the next afternoon as Gary Smalley's words pierced my heart under a bright, cloudless sky against the eastern escarpment of the Rocky Mountains.

Brenda had already told me, but now I was hearing it again. I was a damaging ingredient in my home, and my family deserved better than that. God expected me to listen to her, and it was time I did. I'm glad I acted decisively.

Quiz

Are you responding carefully to your wife's words, or will
   the damage continue?
How long will it be until your marriage looks like it's supposed to?

nagging is her job

But for Adam there was not found a helper meet (suitable, adapted, complementary) for him. And the Lord God caused a deep sleep to fall upon Adam; and while he slept, He took one of his ribs or a part of his side and closed up the [place with] flesh. And the rib or part of his side which the Lord God had taken from the man He built up and made into a woman, and He brought her to the man.

GENESIS 2:20-22, AMP

Behind every nagging wife is a man who will not listen, who will not change, and who will not hear the cry of her heart. Okay, so there are a few exceptions to this statement, but the truth is that your wife's feelings are not a threat but a gift to you.

Yes, I said her feelings are a gift. "Wait a minute, Fred! My wife just told me, 'I don't feel like making love tonight. I don't know why. I just don't!' You call that a gift?"

I sure do. We may not like what she's feeling sometimes—especially on those evenings when we're feeling amorous and she's not—but her ability to sense things that you don't cannot be denied. For instance, your wife's feelings can help you see what you might be doing to block intimacy and oneness, the very intimacy and oneness that can help anchor and defend your sexual purity for good. Besides, if she doesn't express how you could improve yourself, who else is going to do it?

You're like the fellow behind the curtain in *The Wizard of Oz*, manipulating your own awesome image as a majestic, all-knowing, all-wise, fire-breathing wizard. You've fooled nearly everyone in Oz, but your wife is your own personal Toto, nipping at the curtain. She *knows* you're behind that curtain and sees things in you that others don't see or could never see. And no amount of bluster or frantic shouts of "Pay no attention to that man behind the curtain" will diminish her ability to see through your charade.

She *has* to pay attention. How can she allow a fraud to continue? That man behind the curtain is her husband, and she's signed on as his help-mate. Nagging is part of her job description.

No guy, before he gets married, thinks that nagging is part of the package. Up until we exchange our wedding vows, we've been used to living our own lives, often without any interference—or input—from other parties. Then we are pronounced husband and wife, take off for a wonderful honey-moon, and return to live under one roof. We may not know it at the time, but during the first few years of marriage, we are about to undergo prob-ably the fastest period of Christian change and growth at any time in our lives. Call it God's ultimate shakedown cruise.

And who is at the center of this voyage, right at your side and too near your ear? Your helpmate.

"Just doing my job, Captain!"

Her charge from God? To help lift you to Christian greatness, to help you see what you can't see, and to help you change in ways you never thought possible. That sounds pretty nice at first, doesn't it? Christian greatness sounds great to my ears.

But then she begins to notice a few things about you, especially the times you lose your temper or begin trampling her. When she points them out, you become angry or sulk or look for ways to get back at *her*. Whenever Brenda initiated a "discussion" about my behavior toward her or something I had said, I didn't like at all what she had to say. I thought she was a nag, someone getting on my case for trying to show a little leadership in the family. Suddenly, I wished she'd spend a bit more time on her *other* job—like submission to my leadership.

Then when things escalated, and Brenda stuck a finger in my face, I didn't particularly like her attitude. *I'll change when she changes her attitude! She'll just have to go first!*

What? How did I have the right to complain about her attitude when I was punching holes in the dry wall? *I* was the one blowing it because I was trampling Brenda—practically suffocating her and our marriage. Things didn't turn around until I repented of my behavior.

Your helpmate is your greatest asset, and if you are wise, you'll honor that asset like this former marine:

> I have been married to my wife, Michelle, for four years, and we got off to a rocky start. I was married before when I was a young marine, so I've brought a lot of dysfunction, pain, and sin into this marriage. Michelle has a gentle and loving spirit, but she also can be very blunt when it comes to my shortcomings.
>
> I am currently finishing my degree in pastoral ministry and right now do a lot of outreach ministry, but I would be doing none of that were it not for Michelle. She has helped me to confront my sinful attitude, which has played a huge part in giving me the strength and courage to pursue His call on my life.

Over time I learned what this fellow had learned: When Brenda pointed out my failings, she wasn't looking down her nose at me. She knew she didn't deserve to throw the first stone, and her intention was not to judge me at all. As a helpmate, she was not so much pointing a finger at *my* failings but pointing to a wound on us.

That's why when your wife has confronted you six times about the same thing, and you still haven't done anything to change your behavior, she feels you don't care about her. You obviously must not care enough about her to fix something that's hurting the relationship and stunting your Christian growth.

Humble yourself. Accept her role. She's a great helpmate, the special person God had planned for you. If your wife says something, and you don't like the attitude of how she says it, don't demand that she button up, and please don't tell her where to get off.

Instead, *you* button up. *You* pray about it. And while you are at it, listen to her and change!

Quiz

If your wife had to live her life over again, would she choose to marry you again?

If she is on her second marriage, has she done any better this time around in being married to you? Are you a winner, or have her dreams been dashed again?

Someday, as she reflects upon your marriage after your death, will marriage appeal to her again? Why don't you ask her.

it's not about you

If your first concern is to look after yourself, you'll never find your-self. But if you forget about yourself and look to me, you'll find both yourself and me.

MATTHEW 10:39, MSG

In our premarriage classes, Brenda and I used to ask the young couples sit-ting brightly in their chairs, "What do you hope to get out of marriage that you could not get if you stayed single?"

We heard just about every answer under the sun, but many could be distilled down to the promise they would make at the altar: the promise to honor and cherish till death parts them. They were seeking a soul mate who would bring lifetime personal fulfillment—sexually, emotionally, and spiritually.

When we posed the same question to the couples in our young mar-rieds class, the answers weren't soaked in the same starry-eyed optimism. In fact, our question prompted answers that sounded more like marital gripes:

- "We're just so incompatible."
- "He just doesn't respect me."
- "How can I respect her behavior?"
- "I'll start forgiving him when he starts forgiving me!"
- "I'll start treating her better when she starts being happier again!"

What happened? There has been a collision of our lower ways of thinking and God's higher, broader thinking on marriage.

As the heavens are higher than the earth, so are my ways higher than your ways and my thoughts than your thoughts. (Isaiah 55:9)

The blinders are certainly off now! Just a few months earlier many of these couples were convinced that God had personally put two of His wonderful children together in marriage, to live happily ever after in romantic bliss. It was as though He would turn down the marriage bed every night and place a chocolate on the pillow. God would be their quiet, benevolent behind-the-scenes partner in their marriage of three.

But things don't work out that way. God has higher purposes for marriage, and it's not all about you. Let me illustrate this with a story involving my children.

When they were young, each of our four children had assigned chores to do at night, varying according to their ages and abilities. When Michael, our youngest, was a toddler, we staggered the schedules of their chores so they weren't all doing their chores at the same time. This ensured there was always someone free to play with Michael and keep him from gumming up the works.

But Saturday's long, fun days precluded the staggered-chore schedule on Saturday night, so we'd all be working our jobs at the same time, with Michael usually slowing things up or making more messes whenever he attempted to "help out." Most nights I responded by asking Rebecca, the second youngest, to watch Michael while splitting her chores between Jasen and Laura to pick up the slack.

Jasen thought he was getting gypped. "Can't we take turns watching Michael each week?" he asked. "It isn't fair that we have to do Rebecca's chores all the time!"

"I hear you, Son, and I know it may not seem fair to you, but as the dad, I have a lot more to consider than your idea of fairness," I said. Pausing, I grinned, "My ways are higher than your ways, big boy!"

Actually, I *did* have higher ways. Sure, I was concerned with fairness for Jasen, but I had other concerns as well, like what was fair to Rebecca. Had I made Jasen the baby-sitter, his chores would have been too much to handle for Rebecca at her age. That wouldn't have been fair to Rebecca.

I also had to ask what was fair to Michael. Rebecca was his favorite playmate because she was closest to his age, so she was better suited to the task.

And who was committed? When Rebecca baby-sat Michael, she actually stayed and played with him through to the end. When Jasen or Laura baby-sat, they often got bored and wandered off, leaving Michael free to roam and rattle.

Finally, who needed to learn to submit to authority, even when it wasn't fair? Hmm, I wonder?

You see, Jasen's fairness was on my mind, but his fairness could only come through my higher ways of thinking. I wanted fairness for Jasen, but I also wanted what was best for Jasen and what was best for the family.

In response to my little "higher ways" joke, Jasen grunted, "I don't care about all that, Dad. It still isn't fair." (He wasn't being a smart aleck, by the way. He was just being honest.)

In short, he was saying, "Dad, you aren't listening to me! It is so clear that my way is the right way. Why can't you see that as clearly as me?"

His young mind lacked the maturity to grasp the big picture, and it's similar to how we sometimes do not see the big picture regarding the way God designed marriage.

We choose to marry a young woman based on similarities and compatibility. But when the honeymoon's over, we sometimes believe we've made a mistake, not thinking for one moment that God *also* brings us together for our differences, since living happily ever after is not the only thing He has in mind for us. We're blinded and trapped by our less-mature, lower-ways views, as Jasen was.

But God has much more on His mind, and it may not be until all is said and done that we will understand why God brought the two of us together.

When we whine, "God, You aren't listening to me! It is so clear that we're incompatible, and You've made a mistake here. You promised a soul mate, but look what I have instead. It isn't fair! Why did this have to happen to me?" like Jasen, we aren't grasping the big picture. Providing a lifetime soul mate *is* on His list, but how soon we'll *seem* like soul mates on a day-to-day basis depends upon the softness of our hearts to His sanctification work. That's part of God's higher ways.

He wants happiness for you, but He *also* wants what is best for you and what is best for your wife. He knows that these differences will force you to learn to love the unlovely, the very bedrock trait of Christian character.

Of course, in response to my character training, Jasen responded, "I don't care. You are treating Beck better than me, and you don't even care."

We say the same thing to God: "I don't care, Lord! She's impossible, unreasonable, and I can't understand her. And You don't even care! I quit. I'm getting divorced!"

But isn't it caring and right for God to improve your character? You *are* His, after all. Besides, marriage is not all about you. He wants to improve her character through marriage too.

What if God needs to change your wife by making her struggle through these problems with you? Is it not fair for God to ask you to serve Him this way after everything He's done for you? Maybe it isn't always a pleasant task, but serving God like this is far better than going to hell for your sins, don't you think? You owe God a lot for your salvation, and God isn't asking too much of you when He asks you to stick with her and cherish her while He works in her to dump her baggage or to heal some prickly inner pain that's roughing up your relationship. In the last analysis, the bottom line is always the same for any of us: We're never truly a marriage of three until we accept His higher-ways thinking on marriage.

Quiz

Have you learned to submit to God's higher purposes in
   your marriage, even when things don't seem fair and your
   compatibility with her seems to have vanished?
Are you really hers in this marriage?
More important, are you really His?

storm warning

One day Jesus said to his disciples, "Let's cross over to the other side of the lake." So they got into a boat and started out. On the way across, Jesus lay down for a nap, and while he was sleeping the wind began to rise. A fierce storm developed that threatened to swamp them, and they were in real danger.

The disciples woke him up, shouting, "Master, Master, we're going to drown!"

So Jesus rebuked the wind and the raging waves. The storm stopped and all was calm! Then he asked them, "Where is your faith?"

And they were filled with awe and amazement. They said to one another, "Who is this man, that even the winds and waves obey him?"

Luke 8:22-25, NLT

This story has always amazed me (Steve) when I've reflected on what it means in my life, because I've been through my share of big storms. Perhaps you feel the same way, because your life has been one storm after another. After a tiny stretch of calm, up comes another squall that threatens everything that you are and all that you have. If you've traversed a similar course, there are some points to this story from Luke that may help.

The most glaring aspect of this rough-water scenario is that Jesus, knowing full well there would be a storm coming up, told the disciples to get in the boat and get out on the water anyway, deliberately putting everyone into harm's way. The Master of the Universe could have done things differently. For instance, He could have suggested that everyone sit tight on high ground until the storm passed through, thereby teaching them to trust in His prophetic insights. But there were other lessons to teach and learn that day.

Some people have a false belief that once you are walking with Jesus, the storms of life will be rerouted to the other side of the lake or over to some nearby mountain range. They believe that while the lives of non-Christians will be full of misery and heartache, we Christians will be free of rough waters, claiming that our faith in Christ provides protection from the struggles that the rest of the world experiences.

This is not true. Storms will rage in the lives of even the most dedicated Christians. Gale-force winds blow where they will, and sometimes Jesus puts us in the boat to face them, even though He could direct us to stay on shore where we would be safe. But if that happened, we would miss out on the lessons that can only be learned during the upheaval of a major storm.

And He wants us to learn these lessons. He wants to make us normal.

Life's storms have various sources, and sometimes we even bring them on ourselves. Even if you're trying to be God's man, living God's way is especially difficult in this society of pleasure-seeking hedonists, and storms will sometimes blow up out of our own mistakes—our oversized egos, our lack of patience, or our inability to control our anger. Although we hate huge torrents of water crashing against our boat again and again, we don't change course. Sometimes it takes a tidal wave of pain before we finally hand the ship's helm over to God and begin tacking His way.

Other storms are not of our making. God gives free choice to all of us, and some storms blow up from the mistakes of others as their free choices hurt others, including you. Still more storms roll in because we live in a fallen world full of death and disease. Since Adam and Eve fell in the garden, the black storms of death and illness have made this a particularly tough place to live. God does not cause these storms to happen, but He allows them. This is a reality we have no choice but to deal with.

You may be going through a level-five hurricane right now, or your life could even look like a colorful weather map full of rainstorms, tornadoes, thundershowers, and even a hurricane or two brewing in the open waters. Given the reality of your storm map, I hope you're determined to weather them well rather than be weather-beaten.

But if you are being buffeted now, remember that you have hope. If you're one of those who's fortunate to enjoy smooth sailing, please know that the winds will pick up and the seas will roar. When that happens, keep Jesus' words from John 16:33 in mind: "I have told you all this so that you may have peace in me. Here on earth you will have many trials and sorrows. But take heart, because I have overcome the world" (NLT).

That is great news for all of us storm fighters. Trials and sorrows will come no matter how loved or how good or how determined we are, but God is bigger than any of them. He has assured us that He is more powerful than anything that comes our way, so we can go through these storms knowing He will get us through them. After all, that's the whole point of the storm. He wants us changed and standing safely on the other side, that we might shine forth ever more brightly for Him.

Today, if your boat is rocking and sails are ripping and water is splashing overboard, hand the ship's wheel over to Jesus. Keep your faith and tack His way. He will get you through.

Quiz

Are you thanking Him for His grace or drowning in woe and
   chafing over your situation?
Is your storm proving you to be faithful?

plank in the eye

*Why do you look at the speck of sawdust in your brother's eye
and pay no attention to the plank in your own eye?... You hypo-
crite, first take the plank out of your eye, and then you will see
clearly to remove the speck from your brother's eye.*

Luke 6:41-42

Sibling rivalry is *so* pleasant. Upon returning from services one Sunday
evening, Jasen proclaimed a bit too loudly, "I think I did a little bit better
than Laura in church tonight."

He was baiting me, but I didn't bite, so he wiggled the bait a bit more.

"We were all singing, but Laura wasn't singing much."

I couldn't resist that one. Turning to my older son, I asked, "Jasen, why
do you have to win all the time? She was doing the best she could, and even
if she wasn't, I was standing right there. I don't need you to tell me whether
she was singing or not."

"But you didn't say anything to her!"

"That's my business. You just watch yourself and make sure *you* are
doing okay. That's what the Bible means when it says to take the plank out
of your own eye before you worry about the speck in someone else's.
Besides, I have eyes and ears, and I know what Laura was doing. If she's out
of line, I'll take care of it."

It's funny how we fathers can apply that lesson so well to our kids but miss it completely in our own lives.

We'd just finished supper one Saturday night, and after clearing the table, we were sitting back down for a round of devotions. Now, Saturday is payday around the Stoeker house—allowance time. Since it had been a wild day, though, I hadn't yet paid the kids for their weekly chores, nor had I passed the weekly household funds into Brenda's care. Brenda and I have worked out a budget, and she has the responsibility of managing the day-to-day purchases that keep our household running.

As I cracked Scripture and prepared to read, Brenda interrupted, "Can I have the weekly money now? I'd like to put it away while you read."

"No, not while we're doing family devotions."

"Don't treat me like a six-year-old!" she snapped, clearly miffed.

"I'm not, sweetheart. But if I give you the money now, they'll want their allowance now too," I said, nodding toward the kids.

She rolled her eyes, but I ignored her and pressed on.

I began to read, but before long I could hear Brenda reading too. That's right, *hear*. She was moving her lips as she read a novel, whispering ever so slightly as she did so.

"Dear, please don't read that other book while we are doing devotions."

"I'm listening," she replied huffily.

"Right! I can hear you whispering while you're reading!"

She burst out laughing, knowing I'd caught her in the act. She put the book down peacefully and settled in like a good girl.

By this time, however, the rest of the natives were restless. Once again I began to read, only to hear Jasen noisily chomp on a cookie that he'd just soaked in a glass of milk. My temperature was pushing higher.

"Jasen, you know the rules about eating during devotions."

"But, Dad—"

I gave him a withering look, which straightened him out. But my quick victory set a nice big burr under his saddle, and he couldn't let me win that easily. Looking for a softer target, he turned his sights on Laura, who was biding her time by quietly picking at some food stuck between her teeth.

"Laura, that's *so* gross," he whined dramatically. "Don't *do* that while we're trying to have devotions. I can't concentrate!" As if he really cared!

My blood was really simmering now. "Jasen, stop that! And the rest of you, listen up good. I want no more interruptions at this table, or someone's in trouble!"

Jasen just couldn't resist that challenge. He said something smart-alecky, which prompted me to march him to the bathroom for some corrective measures.

By now I'd reached critical mass on the whole devotional thing. Stalking angrily back out of the bathroom, I grabbed Brenda's money out of a bank envelope and rifled it at her like a burst of oversized confetti, declaring, "Devotions are over. I've gotta go." Then I stomped outside for a long walk to cool off. (Brenda and I have agreed that whenever I've reached the end of my fuse, "I've gotta go" is my signal that it would be better for me to leave than to try to continue the conversation.)

About a half hour later, I walked back into the house to survey the damage. Before I could say a word, Brenda rushed to the door and apologized immediately. "Honey, I know I was wrong, and I know I started this whole thing. I don't know what got into me tonight. I think I'm stressed and exhausted."

"That's okay, sweetheart, I understand. And let's face it, I was not exactly Mr. Christian myself tonight. I'm very sorry for losing my temper. But I've still got to tell you that this really hurt me. I was trying to be a spiritual leader tonight, but I didn't get any cooperation from you. It makes it that much harder when you ignore my leadership."

"I know. I thought about it while you were gone, and I knew how hurt you must be. I want so much to support you. I'll try not to do it again."

For many years of our marriage, we couldn't have had such a conversation. Back then I would have launched a wilting attack about that speck in her eye while delivering a couple of sharp low blows for good measure.

For the most part the both of us have learned to express our hurt without retaliation. Now we know that an expression of our feelings needn't be an attack on the other's character. I guess you could say that we're maturing.

That evening, as Brenda and I apologized to each other, I was grateful I sensed some ears listening in from around the corner. You know, we can tell our kids, "Look to your own plank," for years, but sometimes a few illustrations like this can cement these truths in ways that a lecture never could.

Quiz

Are you maturing in your marriage, or are you being driven insane by the same old looping circle of painful communication?

Are you expecting the weather to change without a change in the humility?

Just when is your marriage going to match up to God's dreams?

intimate parenthood

For I have known (chosen, acknowledged) him [as My own], so that he may teach and command his children and the sons of his house after him to keep the way of the Lord and to do what is just and righteous, so that the Lord may bring Abraham what He has promised him.

GENESIS 18:19, AMP

God knew Abraham, choosing him in that place and at that time in history so that Abraham would order his family to follow the Lord in righteousness. Hasn't God known and chosen you for the same purpose?

Sometimes when my firstborn son, Jasen, was toddling around on his little legs, I'd see him grinning and drooling in his innocent way, but my heart would break and tears would flow as I thought about his future.

"Oh, God, isn't there anything I can do for my son?" I'd beg. "Isn't there any way to keep him out of this pit I'm in? Please, Lord, don't let him grow up to be like me!" I ached and groaned at the thought of my precious son trapped by the same addictive porn habits that gripped my grandpa, my dad, and finally me.

I didn't want my son hooked by the likes of Halle Berry and other Hollywood stars who disrobe in their films or ensnared by the nameless nude models in cyberspace. When he looked in the mirror, I didn't want him to feel what I once felt when I looked in the mirror. My sexuality owned me, and I knew it. I couldn't control it, and I didn't want Jasen paying the same price at the same toll bridge that other men in the family had paid.

Recently, a friend told me that when she was praying she saw a father standing before a mirror, but there was no reflection. "This man represented countless fathers, and there was no reflection because of those fathers' sin," she said. "They tried to hide it from God and from their sons, but it ate through their lives.

"There was no reflection and no substance to these fathers. Only emptiness. They had no hope for themselves, and no hope for their sons. They can't give their sons what they need to keep pure because they don't have it themselves."

Nothing I've heard better describes my past feelings of desperation. I was an empty suit—I had no hope and no insight. I knew of no way to lead my son into righteousness. Many nights I'd stare at the ceiling and question God's wisdom in allowing me to be a father at all. I *knew* He could see what I had become. How could He trust me when I kept falling into sexual sin? How could I raise this son of His named Jasen, that wonderful little boy He'd loaned to my home?

Yet I *was* the one chosen by God at this moment in history to become a father to one of His precious lambs. If you're a father, the same is true of you.

I didn't have any experience when our Jasen arrived on the scene. And God certainly knew what my character was like in those days, yet God chose me to raise Jasen. I thought, *I am no Abraham! I don't have the character or purity to do it!* True, but God knew me, choosing me to lead my family after the Lord in righteousness. Sure, there was no reflection and no substance in me because of my sin, but I did have the power of God with me. The question before me was this: Did I love God enough to change my ways and illustrate His name well before Jasen?

It took me some time to become what He knew I could be, but He'd placed the new life in me and trusted me to respond. I owed God dearly for that, and I couldn't afford to dog it in my response.

You owe it to God to illustrate His name beautifully before your children. How far are you willing to go to paint that picture? How open are you willing to be about your life? How committed are you to calling sin, sin and dumping the baggage you have carried into your new life as a dad? Gratefully, now that you are on this side of purity, you see more clearly than ever that you have no right to stay the same wherever you're missing the Lord's mark. You must walk normally like Christ and listen well to the Spirit so that you can complete the task at hand.

you are a proverb

And you shall become an astonishment, a proverb, and a byword among all nations where the LORD will drive you.

DEUTERONOMY 28:37, NKJV

My friend Dave Johnson and I were casually shooting the breeze one Sunday morning in the church foyer, waiting for our families to catch up with us. After a brief pause in the conversation, Dave switched directions. "Hey, I've been meaning to ask you something. Do you know Cathy Bergen?"

"No, I don't think so. Should I?"

"You bet," Dave said enthusiastically. "She's been coming to church for about a year. Jill met her when they worked together on a project during the missions convention. We've just loved getting to know her."

"Why?"

"Well, I don't know. She's just a real Karen Corsen–type."

Ah. That's all it took.

If Cathy Bergen was anything like St. Karen Corsen, then I would instantly like her. It was a high honor to be dubbed a Karen Corsen–type. That meant you were kind, compassionate, and your passion for Jesus was evident to anyone who met you. In other words, Karen was a proverb for someone whose character shone brightly for Christ.

The word *proverb* has two meanings. You're probably familiar with the first—a short, pithy saying that expresses a well-known truth. King Solomon, the wisest man who ever lived, wrote three thousand proverbs.

The other meaning of *proverb* is not as well known: someone who is recognized as a typical example. That's what Dave was doing when he called Cathy Bergen a real Karen Corsen–type.

Early in my marriage I was budding into a *bad* proverb, especially in the way I was treating the kids. I just couldn't see it, however. Brenda couldn't help but notice, of course, which meant she would make sure *I* heard about it too.

"Fred, you are just being too harsh with the kids when you get after them," she said one day for the umpteenth time. This speech of hers was getting really annoying.

I defended myself. "I've told you a million times, would you *please* quit holding me to your female standards? I play a different role than you do: Fathers are *supposed* to be stronger. I approach parenting differently than you do. You just don't understand that the kids need a father's strong hand."

"They need a *strong* hand, but not a harsh one. There's a difference."

"A minor difference. Pure semantics."

"It's not semantics," she barked back. "There's a major difference! The kids are scared of you."

"Oh, come now," I laughed derisively. "Don't overdramatize. That just isn't the case, and you know it. Kids are smart. All kids know that fathers are different, and they have no trouble accepting that. Besides, it makes them feel more secure to have a strong hand and tight boundaries. Scared? No way."

I proposed a little test. "If you think you know so much, let's sit the kids down and ask *them* what they think about our parenting skills. Do you have the courage to do that?"

That was an arrogant question, although I didn't know it at the time. I thought my idea was brilliant, a proposal born of Solomon's wisdom. What a simple way to help my poor blind wife see the truth and bring an immediate end to this parenting battle once and for all.

We sat the kids down in a row on our bed, legs dangling and kicking restlessly. Jasen was around nine years old; Laura, seven; and Rebecca, about four. I began by asking what they thought of the way Mom was raising them. I couldn't draw a single negative remark from them. I even suggested some possibilities to them, but they all responded in turn, saying, "No, Mommy is not like that."

I tacked to a different course. "Kids, now I need your help on something else. You know I want to be the best dad I can be for you, right?"

"Yeah, we know that, Daddy," said Laura.

"Well, I have something I want to ask you about me, and I want you to feel free to tell the truth, okay?"

"Okay, Daddy, we'll tell you the truth," Jasen said brightly.

"Well, Mommy and Daddy have been talking, and Mom thinks that maybe I'm too harsh when I get after you about doing something wrong. Do you think she's right? Just feel free to tell the truth. We really need to know."

"What's *harsh* mean, Daddy?" asked my cherub Rebecca.

"It means he growls real hard, like this," Jasen piped in and then scrunched up his face and snarled.

"Thank you, Jasen," I said, rolling my eyes. "Actually, Rebecca, it means that sometimes I really get after you when you do things wrong, because I want to help you learn quickly so you don't do it again. Mommy thinks I scare you when I'm doing that."

"Oh, okay. Yeah, Daddy, sometimes you really scare me when you do that," she replied.

"Daddy, you can really look mean, and sometimes it hurts my feelings," Laura said.

"You really scare me, too, Dad," added Jasen. "Sometimes it bothers me all night when you get like that."

My children—my flesh and blood—were too young to sugarcoat the truth and too naive to lie about their feelings. Inside, I was stricken to the point of tears. Outside, my only thought was to set them straight. I snapped, "I wouldn't need to be so harsh if you wouldn't keep doing the same things wrong all the time. If you're scared, it's your fault, not mine." After that missile launch, I glared at them and stormed angrily from the room.

Case closed—in Brenda's favor.

What would your kids say if they had the freedom to tell the truth about your parenting style or the way you act around them? What has your wife already pointed out over and over again, only to have her message jammed at the source by your closed spirit?

Humble yourself and ask them. Take it from me, it only hurts for a while. Besides, the pain can be a good thing if it leads to a timely change. You may even become a wonderful proverb to your children.

Quiz

What kind of proverb are you around the house?

How about around the church?

Do your proverbs match up, or are you faking somewhere?

there will be a day

And he brought him to Jesus. Jesus looked at him and said, "You are Simon son of John. You will be called Cephas" (which, when translated, is Peter).

JOHN 1:42

What do you love? You will certainly become *what* you love. Do you love holiness? Then you will become holy. Do you love the Word of God? Then you will become like Christ, the living Word. Do you love the name of Jesus? Then your life will manifest His name before all men.

On the day that Peter met Jesus, he was just another passionate man whose emotions curled and crashed like the waves of the sea, ebbing and flowing with the tides of his life. He had sworn that he would not deny that he knew Jesus, but on the eve of His death, Peter chickened out and claimed he never knew the man.

So why in the world did Jesus call him "Rock"? (Both Cephas [Aramaic] and Peter [Greek] mean "rock.") Because He knew what this apostle would become—stable, sure, brave, and trustworthy.

Peter became that rock on the Day of Pentecost, standing up and boldly proclaiming:

"Therefore let all Israel be assured of this: God has made this Jesus, whom you crucified, both Lord and Christ."

When the people heard this, they were cut to the heart and said to Peter and the other apostles, "Brothers, what shall we do?" (Acts 2:36-37)

What has Jesus called you? Jesus has called you chosen (see Ephesians 1:11). He has called you holy and dearly loved (see Colossians 3:12), His fellow heir (see Galatians 3:29), and His faithful follower (see Revelation 17:14). He has called you sanctified (see 1 Corinthians 6:11).

Do you love Jesus? Then you will become these things, but only as you discover the secret of John the Baptist, that same John that Jesus called the greatest man ever born of women (see Matthew 11:11).

What's the secret?

He must increase, but I must decrease. (John 3:30, NKJV)

As you manifest the name of Jesus, shining forth and illustrating His name in your life, your own colors and tones must decrease while the colors and tones of Jesus must increase.

I noticed this happening in my life one day when Brenda and I were riding bikes at sunset along a trail that wends its way through the trees and grasses of the flood plain near our home. We'd been gliding silently through the dimming light so as not to frighten any nearby deer, when suddenly Brenda's excited exclamation startled me: "Hey, you got the highest of compliments today!"

"Really?" My ears perked up.

"Yeah, really," she smiled. "Remember how Rebecca said last night that she wished we could go canoeing with the Stracks again?"

Now I was smiling. Ron and Sandy Strack were some of the best friends we'd ever had, and we'd been missing them horribly since they'd moved to Champaign, Illinois. Ron had been named senior pastor of a church there. Our families went on picnics and canoe rides and did all the crazy things that families do together on lazy summer weekends in Iowa. When they left, they took a lot of our fun with them.

Rebecca and I had been lamenting our loss the night before, and she wondered if we could find a river between Des Moines and Champaign where we could meet with canoes and swimsuits and picnic baskets. But between my book deadlines and Ron's preaching schedule, it became clear that our chances were pretty slim.

Not to be denied, Rebecca had another idea. "Mom, if we can't find a time with the Stracks, why not find a family around here to go? We know many families we could go with."

She was right. We belong to a large church with dozens of families, many of whom we had done family-fun activities with over the last twenty years. "Well," said Brenda. "Who did you have in mind?"

"How about the Simpsons?"

"No, Gil hurt his back recently, so he won't be up to canoeing for quite a while."

Rebecca would not be deterred. "Then how about the Billingsleys?"

"Nope, I don't think so," Brenda said. "Sue hates bugs and dirt and all that outdoor stuff."

Jasen, who had been following the conversation, knew just the right family. "How about the Browns?"

"Now *that's* a good idea! Your dad really likes Gray and Heather."

"Oh, I'm not sure I like that idea," Rebecca piped up.

"Me, either," said Michael. "Their dad scares me."

"Me, too," said Rebecca. "He can be so sharp in the way he speaks to his kids. He jerked Andy's arm and called him a stupid idiot the other day, and Andy hadn't really done anything."

"Yeah, he's been really harsh to us sometimes too," Laura said. "I just don't know how fun that would be, Mom. I'd be afraid all day that I'd bump his canoe and he'd flip out."

"Well, maybe you're right, kids," Brenda conceded. "I've also seen that in Gray. I guess we'll have to think of another family then."

There was a pause in the conversation as everyone turned back to the family search...everyone but Jasen, that is. His mind was musing in a different direction.

"Dad used to be harsh too, didn't he, Mom?" he asked.

And there it was—*used to be.* That was likely the highest compliment I'll ever receive from a family member. That meant my days of harsh rule had been over for some time, and my kids knew the difference.

I had been transformed, just as Peter had been when Jesus called him Rock, knowing that Peter had the character necessary for him to build His church on His foundation.

For the first half of my marriage, I could have been named "Harsh Stoeker" for the way I came down on everybody in the family. But Jesus called me sanctified, and when He came into my life and began working on my attitude, my character, and my demeanor, that harshness melted away. You could say that my Harsh decreased and my Jesus increased.

Quiz

What name might your wife and kids call you when you're not around?

You wouldn't necessarily know without asking. Are you man enough to ask your wife about it?

Are you still living up to that name, or are you getting rid of it through grace and change?

how far will you go for God?

*So if you consider me a partner, welcome him as you would wel-
come me. If he has done you any wrong or owes you anything,
charge it to me.... Confident of your obedience, I write to you,
knowing that you will do even more than I ask.*

PHILEMON 17-18,21

These weren't just flattering words from Paul. He knew Philemon, and he
knew his close friend would do even more than he asked of him. Paul was
aware that Philemon's love for him was that great.

Does God know this about you? Could He brag about you like that?
"Hey, I'm very confident of his obedience. I know that he will do even
more than I ask."

During the oil shocks of the 1970s, lawmakers responded by cutting the
speed limit on our nation's freeways from sixty-five to fifty-five miles an
hour to conserve gasoline. My father threw a fit. He was a traveling sales-
man, and the slower speed would cost him a lot of time, and after all, time *is*
money. He vowed immediately that he would not obey these laws. Though
I was still in high school at the time, I can still remember his words.

"Freddie, traffic laws are only here to protect the poor drivers. I've literally driven over a million miles in my day, and I'm a very good driver. But this slow speed puts me to sleep behind the wheel. I'm just not as alert, so this new speed limit will make *me* a poor driver, too."

"Right, Dad," I said, trying to see his point.

"Really, these slower speed limits might as well be a death sentence for me, and I'm not going to let them kill me," he said passionately. "It's literally life and death, me against them. I'm going to buy the best equipment money can buy to get around their radars and speed traps. It's not breaking the law if they don't catch me."

Riding shotgun with Dad—clipping along at eighty miles per hour—made for a tense ride. We'd strain our ears to hear CB transmissions of enemy trooper movements and constantly monitor the early warning radar detection system on his dash. Rather than simply follow the law, Dad spent thousands of dollars over the years to break it.

Later, after we had both became Christians, I pointed out this scripture to Dad one day:

> For rulers hold no terror for those who do right, but for those who do wrong. Do you want to be free from fear of the one in authority? Then do what is right and he will commend you. For he is God's servant to do you good. (Romans 13:3-4)

"Dad, why don't you just do the right thing here? You could relax and not have to be looking in your rearview mirror or watching the Fuzzbuster all the time."

"Son, these people are evil, trying to take my money on speeding tickets to fund their governments. I'm not going to obey evil men. God doesn't expect me to go that far."

Contrast this to the story my pastor told about his father one Sunday morning. One time when he was still a boy, he was napping in the backseat as his dad, a pastor himself, drove south from Pennsylvania, anxious to get to their vacation destination in warmer climes.

Back then the interstate system was incomplete, which meant that many two- and four-lane highways passed through the smallish cities dotting the maps of Rand McNally.

Late one afternoon they passed through yet another unfamiliar city. Searching hard for the correct turn for the road out of town, his dad accidentally ran right through an intersection before seeing the stoplight. The kids were asleep, and his wife didn't notice. No harm was done. No cop was around to enforce things. So what did he do?

He stopped at the nearest gas station to ask directions to the police station, and then drove over to turn himself in. By this time, my pastor was wide awake, and when his dad parked in front of the police station, he scrambled out of the car to go in with him to see what would happen.

As his dad stepped up to the main desk, he informed the duty officer, "Sir, I'm traveling through on my vacation today, and since I'm unfamiliar with your town, I inadvertently ran a red light a few moments ago. I'm here to turn myself in and to make it right."

The officer, a bit startled, replied, "What do you expect me to do, sir?"

As he pulled out his wallet, John's father said, "Well, there must be a fine I can pay, right? If so, I'm here to pay it."

Scratching his head a moment, the officer paused to think. Then smiling kindly, he looked up and said, "Sir, I'm sorry, but we can't fine you for that. We didn't see you do it and, to be honest, I wouldn't know exactly how to fill out the report. But I want to thank you for dropping by, just the same. In all my years on the force, I've never seen anything like this. Good day, sir, and have a great vacation. Drive safely now."

A kook? Before you answer, take a look again at the whole picture.

My father produced three children. All three of us were rebellious to the rules, and we abused alcohol and were promiscuous in college. All three of us turned our backs on God, though we'd spent many summers in Vacation Bible School and attended church on Sundays.

My pastor's father also produced three children. All three are model citizens who've invested themselves in full-time Christian ministry.

Does your obedience to traffic laws affect your success as a father? Not directly, I suppose, but what about the pattern of attitudes represented here? One man did as he pleased. One man was happy to do even more than the Lord asked, so great was his hunger to please Him. What a picture.

Consider this scripture:

I have manifested Your name to the men whom You have
given Me out of the world. They were Yours, You gave them
to Me, and they have kept Your word. Now they have known
that all things which You have given Me are from You.
(John 17:6-7, NKJV)

Jesus was with His disciples for the last time when He said this, and He was reporting back to the Father about what He had accomplished in His short ministry.

Before Jesus left heaven, He was charged to manifest the Father's name before the people. This means "to shine forth" His name, not so much by preaching it, but by living it out and illustrating it. In other words, Jesus was saying, "I've lived out Your nature before them, Father. I've pictured it, and now they understand the truth and they know that I'm from You."

We have that same call from our Father in this world. We, too, are to live out His nature before our world and to illustrate God's love before our wives and children.

Have you shined forth, manifesting His name before your wife? Does she love the Father more because of what she sees in you? Can your kids hardly wait to meet Jesus themselves because of what they see in you—tenderness, gentleness, and kindness?

I sure hope so.

Quiz

Paul knew Philemon's character and knew what he could
   trust him to be and to do. What do your wife and kids
   know about your character?

Do they know for a fact that you will do even more for God
   than He asks, like Philemon?

Are you a man of valor? Do you have the courage to ask
   them?

daring devos

Only be careful, and watch yourselves closely so that you do not forget the things your eyes have seen or let them slip from your heart as long as you live. Teach them to your children and to their children after them.

DEUTERONOMY 4:9

You need to strengthen relationships with those you love the most to cement your victory over sexual sin. The best way to strengthen weak family relationships is to go deep with them, and by that, I mean talk with them and open up your life to them. Let them see your flaws as well as your fine points.

You may think, *It's too late! Besides, I'm no good at opening up like that.* You would be wrong. If there is anything truly immortal on this earth, it is the undying love of a child for his father, no matter how badly that father has botched things up. Your son or daughter still longs for deeper connection with you, regardless of how things look now. We *all* need that connection with our fathers, and if given half the chance, we will seek it to the very end.

If you're still insisting that you're no good at this, all I can say is practice makes perfect. Besides, we're not talking rocket science here. We're talking about sharing a topic no one knows more about—you and the stories of your life. Anyone can do that, and it's really easier to do than I ever thought it would be.

I describe how to go deep in greater detail in another book in this series called *Preparing Your Son for Every Man's Battle.* Fathers can go deep by swapping stories as they go through books with them.

I've found that family devotions are another great place to go deep with your kids. And this exercise naturally leads to deeper relationships with your children—if you open up your life to them.

Have family devotions—a time when you all read and discuss something from the Bible and share prayer requests—lost their appeal to your kids as they've gotten older? When our kids were young, we memorized Scripture, read Bible stories, sang fun songs, and even threw out trivia questions, which helped them learn about the Bible.

But once Jasen and Laura hit their teens, we found that when we would announce, "Time for devotions," groans sometimes arose from the cheap seats.

"I've heard all those old Bible stories!"

"I have schoolwork to do."

"I know all the trivia already!"

Obviously, Brenda and I needed to mix things up. We decided to spend more time telling stories about ourselves—or on ourselves—and the more embarrassing the better, as far as our children were concerned. But you know what? Each story prompted a spiritual lesson to break out—and fascinating discussions between us and the kids.

Any such story instantly became the evening special on our devotional menu that night. The kids, of course, love the evening specials. All I have to do, for instance, is stand in the center of the house and call out, "Hey, kids! Mom has a story for devotions tonight."

Are there groans from the cheap seats? Are you kidding? They love to hear their mother tell one on herself.

"What did Mommy do this time?" they press gleefully. It's an awful lot of fun. Brenda just rolls her eyes with a smile, saying, "You're all going to love this one."

I'll never forget *this* whopper Brenda told on herself. "My story begins when I came out after Sunday church and told Fred, 'I had the worst limburger at church today!'"

The kids immediately started cracking up. "Having limburger" is a Stoekerism based on an old joke my pastor shared from the pulpit years ago. The short version is that there was a man who had fallen asleep on the park bench, and wherever he went the next day, whether it was the coffee shop with its rich aromas, the perfume shop with its expensive fragrances, or the fine flower shop with its bouquets of delicate flowers, he'd say, "Ugh. That smells awful!"

He believed the awful smells were caused by everyone else. Turns out, a friend had pulled a joke on him, wiping a bit of limburger cheese on the man's mustache while he slept. So while our hero thought that he had superior nasal insight, in reality he himself was the one stinking things up.

She told us that she stunk things up when she looked around the church on this particular Sunday morning and remembered some hurt or irritation that each person had done to irk her.

"Like what?" asked one of the girls.

Brenda ticked down the list of names for us one by one and expressed the dark little limburger thoughts she had for each. With each name the laughter rose higher because the whole thing was so ludicrous. After all, this was turning out to be quite a large hunk of smelly cheese.

Of course, there was a serious side as well. Brenda told us how she later repented to the Lord in tears, admitting that her own attitudes were the real sin that morning. The kids were touched deeply by that. We also brought the discussion back to Scripture for teaching purposes, asking questions like, "Michael, how would you have acted differently?" or "Jasen, how can we know it's our own limburger sooner next time?"

Sometimes the kids have a great response, and they back it with Scripture. Sometimes they have to admit that they would have felt or done the very same things themselves. Other times one child might say, "Oh, I had something like that happen to me!" When that happens, we all enjoy a second helping of the evening special as they admit their own fault.

Brenda is superb at this. One evening she said, "I've been thinking about the things we do and don't do in our lives. In this house, we've chosen not to watch sensual movies, not to dress immodestly, and not to drink alcohol. I've always seen these as sacrifices for the Lord, but lately I've been wondering about that. After all, what do they really cost me? It hasn't been that difficult to do because I was raised this way. I've never watched raunchy movies anyway, so not seeing them isn't a big deal. I've never drunk, so that hasn't been a big deal either. But then I got to thinking about the bad things I do all the time, and I haven't tried to stop them at all."

Question marks appeared on every face: *What bad things does Mom do wrong all the time?*

Reading their minds, Brenda smiled. "When I start to tell you about this bad thing, you'll know where I'm heading before I finish the sentence. It's no secret. You know how I complain whenever we have company?"

Laura burst out laughing. "Yes, you always say it's too much work."

"Yes, it is hard work, and with my thyroid condition, I can get so, so tired. But I realized something for the first time a few days ago, and I've been thinking."

"What's that, Mom?" Laura asked.

"You know how the Bible lists the gifts of the Holy Spirit? He gives those gifts to Christians so that they can serve God's people. I've looked at those lists, and there is only one gift listed that I'm certain I have. It's the gift of hospitality, and I know Jesus gave me this gift to serve Him, which caused me to ask myself a question: Can it be right for me to complain every time I get to use the very gift He gave me to serve Him?"

Eyes got big, and no one said a peep.

"I'll answer it for you," Brenda said bravely. "It's totally wrong of me. It is sin, yet I do it all the time and never even address it. See, I'm quick to avoid bad movies—it costs me nothing! But what about complaining when company is coming over? I've been slow as molasses in dealing with this, because it will really cost me to do something about it. I know I'll have to keep a good attitude even when I'm tired."

The kids nodded their understanding. Then Brenda reminded them that we were having houseguests the following week. "I want you to watch me closely to see how I do this time. I've committed my heart to change," she said.

I noticed that the kids watched Brenda when our houseguests arrived, but this time around, she was beyond magnificent.

Quiz

Are you telling stories about yourself to your children—the good, the bad, and the ugly?

Your stories, mixed with God's Word, bring to your kids encounters with God and His truth. Do you have planned, regular times in your home for such encounters with God?

dad on parade

Fix these words of mine in your hearts and minds; tie them as symbols on your hands and bind them on your foreheads. Teach them to your children, talking about them when you sit at home and when you walk along the road, when you lie down and when you get up.

DEUTERONOMY 11:18-19

I used to wonder how I could accomplish Moses' directive from the Old Testament. Like most families, my kids and I lead busy lives. We don't sit around home, nor do we walk or work together very much, unless you count shopping in the malls as a walk. Our culture is vastly different from that of the ancient Hebrews.

And that's perfectly fine. God understands the fast-paced society in which we live, but He still wants us to teach our kids how we apply Scripture to our day-to-day lives. Since our kids aren't with us much during the day to *see* how we apply Scripture, fulfilling this call won't look the same today as it did back then.

That's why we need to do the next best thing, which is to *tell* them what happened during our days, our weeks, our years, to show them how we live Scripture daily. That will fix God's Word in their hearts. They will see how it works. They will get it.

To make this happen, however, means that you will have to share your mistakes along with your successes. Still, I'll admit that this kind of sharing is great fodder for effective family devotions. Not to mention that my children *love* to hear stories about King Dad bumbling through life.

One night I started out devotions by saying, "You know how I was late home from Omaha last night for supper?" I saw a few nods. "My last appointment was running late, and when I ran into a big interstate repair project, the bottleneck drove me bonkers. By the time I got past it, I was just crazy to get home. Anyway, I wasn't really going any faster than usual, but I was in such a hurry that I really didn't slow down too much on the exit ramp at Eighty-Sixth Street."

I could see that the kids were still with me.

"You know how that ramp splits into two lanes up near the lights?" I continued. "Well, you can turn left from both lanes, and I was looking for the shortest one. The left lane was lined way back with cars, but the right lane was empty. So I set my sights to grab the right lane once I reached the split.

"As I approached that Y on the fly, an SUV traveling way too slow was nearing the Y as well. Closing in on him from behind, I needed to know which way he was going. While he was still aiming right up the middle, it looked to me like he'd be heading into the left lane, so I rolled right with all jets blazing," I said, demonstrating with my hands how it happened.

"At that moment, the other driver glanced into his rearview mirror. Startled by my approach, he hit his brakes with a jolt. Now it was my turn to panic, swerving sharply into the right lane and barely missing him. Breathing a deep sigh of relief, I proceeded up to the front row at the light.

"Glancing into my own mirror, I noticed he'd gunned his SUV right up to my tail. As the light turned green, I accelerated to turn left. He stayed right on my bumper, so I could tell he was ticked. A classic case of road rage."

Jasen nodded. As the only driver among the four children, he knew what road rage was.

I powered forward. "I was tired and didn't want to deal with it. I knew he was trying to pass me so he could flip me off, so I got a bit spunky and decided to have a little fun with him. As luck would have it, the cars were spaced just perfectly so that, for two whole miles, I could swerve from lane to lane so that he never quite had the room to get up and pass me. He was right on my tail the whole way, of course, but I wasn't mad. I was giggling, in fact. What a moron!"

"Yeah, he was crazy, Dad," said my youngest, Michael.

"You're right, big guy. When I got to the light to Sixty-Second Avenue, I had to turn right toward Johnston. I figured he'd just head on straight in the left lane. As he tore up next to me, I was just beginning my right turn on red, so I didn't see his face. I thought I'd won our game."

I could tell the kids were hanging on every word. "But to my shock," I continued, "it wasn't over. From the left lane, he ripped a right turn, swerving dangerously in front of me to block my way forward. He flung his door open to attack me. Instead, I made this spectacular swerve out and around him and blasted off down the road. It was really cool, like a movie. Again, it happened so fast I didn't really see him, and I was a half-mile down the road when I looked in the rearview mirror and saw him shaking his fist.

"I slowed down to thirty-five for the remaining short ride home. Glancing casually once more into the rearview mirror, I now saw our little SUV roaring about eighty miles per hour after me. Instantly, I realized this wasn't ever going to be over. No matter how far I drove, he was going to follow me. What if I drove home and he did something to one of you or to the house?"

"Man, Dad, that's scary!" Michael asked.

"Well, you can bet that thought made me mad as a hornet. Suddenly, the giggling was over. Now my family was at risk, and I'd simply had it with this nut. I wasn't about to drive home now, so I decided to turn into the Pioneer Hi-Bred parking lot, which gave him one more chance to back off.

If he went on straight, fine. I'd look at his silly finger and let him go. But if he turned into the parking lot after me, I would get out of my car and give him a pasting he would not soon forget."

"You were going to fight him?" Jasen asked with huge eyes. He couldn't believe that he was hearing his dad say this.

"Yes, I would have, Son. In fact, I have to admit I was so mad by then that I was hoping it would come to that. I turned into the parking lot, and he came right after me, squealing tires. Then he rushed past me and slammed on his brakes to cut me off. Fine! He was going to be sorry he didn't keep on going! I flung my door open and got out of the car and rushed toward his door. He did the same and jumped out with his balled-up fists. Then we both froze. It was Tim Tompkins from church."

The kids gasped, followed by peals of horrified laughter.

"Who's Tim Tompkins?" Rebecca asked. She wasn't sure.

"Tim once attended my premarriage class, and he's been around the church for years. Anyway, we were absolutely speechless in that parking lot, I have to tell you."

"Daddy, what did you do next?" Rebecca squealed, while the others groaned at the spot I was in.

"We both looked down, and then our eyes met again. I said, 'Tim, would you pray with me?' We grabbed hands and I prayed, 'Dear God, we are so, so sorry. We are so ashamed, and we are not worthy to be called Your children. Please forgive us right now and make this experience be a memory between us that binds us rather than separates us. We love You, Lord, and we are Yours.'"

Can you imagine the discussion my children and I had after *that* story? It was great, and you can do the same as well. Tell them about your mistakes, the moronic things you said to your supervisor—or about the times you witnessed lousy behavior. It will give your kids a chance to really know you and give you the opportunity to teach them to do better.

Quiz

Are you teaching your children from your experiences as you walk along the way? If not, how are you fixing His words into the hearts and minds of your children? What is your plan?

loving God

We wait for you; your name and renown are the desire of our hearts. My soul yearns for you in the night; in the morning my spirit longs for you.

ISAIAH 26:8-9

It was Monday evening, and we'd just finished devotions with the family. I'd sent the other three kids upstairs to be tucked into bed by Mom, keeping Jasen downstairs for a little father-son talk.

The night before in church, thirteen-year-old Jasen had spent more time creating a paper chain out of church-pew sundries than listening to the youth pastor, who was speaking that night at our fall back-to-school rally.

On this particular evening we began with some Bible readings followed by a few worship songs. Jasen sat with his legs curled under him, leaning heavily against a pillow and barely singing in the midst of his lazy distraction.

To break his lethargic spell, I shifted gears and asked him to close us in prayer. One by one, he prayed for good grades, safety on the streets, his allergies, and my stress at work…all good things to be sure, but something was missing. I needed to talk to him about it; hence the reason I asked him to stay behind while his siblings trooped off to bed.

"Jasen, do you really love God?" I asked.

"Yes, I do."

"How would you prove that to someone? What evidence is there in your life that you love God?"

"I'm really good, and I always try to do the right thing," Jasen said.

"That's great, and I agree that you do. What else would you say?"

"I read my Bible and obey what it says," he offered.

"That's great too. God wants us to be obedient. In fact, the Bible itself calls obedience great evidence of your love for Him. Jesus said, 'Whoever has my commands and obeys them, he is the one who loves me.' But that isn't all there is. What else would you say?"

"I work hard in school, and I treat my sisters well."

"True enough, but that's obedience again. What else besides obedience?"

"I respect you and listen to you and Mom," he said hopefully.

"Yes, you do honor us as the commandment says, but that's obedience again. What else besides obedience?"

"I always—oops," he stopped. "That's obedience again too." He paused a moment to think. "It seems that everything I think of is obedience!"

"That's great insight, Son. Let's take our eyes off you for a moment and just look at this in general. What else besides obedience is a sign of our love of God in the Bible? Think about the scriptures you know. What else does God desire?"

"Sacrifice?" he asked.

"Hey, that's pretty good. But the Bible says that obedience is better than sacrifice, remember? You are already great at obedience. Can you think of anything that might rank higher than obedience? Anything at all?"

He stared at the floor, now very puzzled. "Dad, I can't think of anything else."

"Jasen, what does God desire from you? No, wait a minute. Let's look at it from another angle. What do *I* desire from you as your father?"

"For me to do the right thing."

"Yes, I desire that so much, because I love the peace that brings to this house and what a great example you set for the other kids. Your obedience means the world to me. But is peace all that I want from you, Son?"

He had no answer.

"Son, when I come in from work, and you are quietly reading a book in the living room, I have peace, and if it happens that you are reading the Bible, so much the better. But I long for something more."

"What is it you want, Dad?"

"I desire you. I long to have you put the book down and get that twinkle in your eye, that one that says you're happy to see me. I long for your hug. And do you know what? That hardly ever happens."

I paused. He was silent.

"And do you know what else? I want you to tell me how unique and special I am, and that you couldn't be happier to call me your dad. And that is what God wants from you too. He loves to see you reading your Bible. But He wants you to put it down once in a while and look up at Him with a smile. He wants to see that tear in your eye as you wonder at His greatness. That's worship. That's telling Him how much you love Him."

"Dad...I didn't know I was like that," he stammered.

"That's what dads are for, Son. My heavenly Daddy is always telling me things I don't know about myself too."

"You mean like how you aren't very friendly to those who you don't really know that well?" he asked.

I chuckled. "Bingo, big guy. He just showed me that one."

"Well, *I'm* friendly to people," he said, defending himself a moment.

"I know, Son. You really are. It's kind of funny. *I'm* friendly to God, but not very friendly to people. *You* are friendly to people, but not so friendly to God. We both have some learning to do, don't we?" I said, grinning.

What is the end game of obedience? Intimacy. That's what He wants.

He knows that Christ's death has restored you to His garden forevermore. Now He wants you to love Him, so He can walk with you in the cool of the day. So that you can gaze into His face in wonder, and He can see your passion for Him and all that He is. He takes great delight in you, and He longs after you. He loves you.

Quiz

Does your spirit long after God?
Is His name and renown the desire of your heart?
Isn't it time to go all out in seeking His face?

Steve can be reached by e-mail at sarterburn@newlife.com

Fred can be reached by e-mail at fred@stoekergroup.com
or at www.fredstoeker.com.

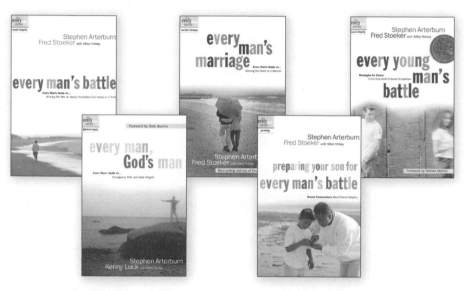

every man's battle workshops

from New Life Ministries

new Life Ministries receives hundreds of calls every month from Christian men who are struggling to stay pure in the midst of daily challenges to their sexual integrity and from pastors who are looking for guidance in how to keep fragile marriages from falling apart all around them.

As part of our commitment to equip individuals to win these battles, New Life Ministries has developed biblically based workshops directly geared to answer these needs. These workshops are held several times per year around the country.

- Our workshops **for men** are structured to equip men with the tools necessary to maintain sexual integrity and enjoy healthy, productive relationships.

- Our workshops **for church leaders** are targeted to help pastors and men's ministry leaders develop programs to help families being attacked by this destructive addiction.

Some comments from previous workshop attendees:

"An awesome, life-changing experience. Awesome teaching, teacher, content and program." —DAVE

"God has truly worked a great work in me since the EMB workshop. I am fully confident that with God's help, I will be restored in my ministry position. Thank you for your concern. I realize that this is a battle, but I now have the weapons of warfare as mentioned in Ephesians 6:10, and I am using them to gain victory!" —KEN

"It's great to have a workshop you can confidently recommend to anyone without hesitation, knowing that it is truly life changing. Your labors are not in vain!" —DR. BRAD STENBERG, Pasadena, CA

If sexual temptation is threatening your marriage or your church, please call **1-800-NEW-LIFE** to speak with one of our specialists.

start a bible study
and connect with others
who want to be God's man.

Every Man Bible Studies are designed to help you discover, own, and build on convictions grounded in God's word. Available now in bookstores.